FOREVER 25

a Mother's Journey through Grief

by Shelley Tucker

Forever 25: A Mother's Journey Through Grief
by Shelley Tucker *(also known as Ixchel Tucker)*

Edited by Edward Mason

Forever25.us

Dedicated to my son,

Gabriel Guzman.

Author's Note

I've told this story from my memories, as the events and experiences have unfolded in my life. As such, my memories aren't exact. Some events have been combined and timelines may be off and the exact accounting of how things happened may not match up with those of others in my story. But rather than clarifying every detail to match perfectly with my family and friends, I've written from simply my perspective and the impact these experiences have had on me.

Conversations are from memory and my point of view. Some of the actual names have been changed to protect anonymity.

I apologize for any errors to the actual facts. I also apologize to all my friends and family that are a part of my life and those included in this memoir for any misrepresentations that may have inadvertently occurred.

Shelley Tucker

*"I can fly, but I want your wings." from the
song Angel Gabriel, by Lamb*

*"God changes caterpillars into butterflies,
sand into pearls, and coal into diamonds. Using
time and pressure he's working on you, too." -
Rick Warren*

TABLE OF CONTENTS

Prologue

JULY 2007. I was sitting at Naty's Restaurant, looking out the main road, Calle Revolución. It was a normal day in Tepoztlán, where I lived in Central Mexico. Lunch at Naty's was our usual routine. My partner, Roberto, sat reading USA Today, the only paper he could get in town with US and world news, while I waited for our food.

When Roberto left to visit the men's room I glanced over at the paper. As I scanned, with pretend interest, my eyes stuck on a headline, something about George W Bush extending *"Stop Loss"* to US Troops. I grabbed the paper and continued reading. It was saying that enlisted men that were serving a tour in Iraq or Afghanistan would be required to stay another three months.

When Roberto returned I showed it to him. "How can they do this?" I asked.

My son, Gabe, was in the Army. He had shipped off to Afghanistan in February. He was supposed to be there for one full year. According to this article he might have to stay three more months.

I had to know more. I emailed Gabe and he wrote back. Yes, this applied to him and his company.

I questioned him more in September, on his last visit home. He said it was unavoidable. There was nothing they could do.

On March 8, 2008 he was killed in action, two months after he should have been home and one month before the rest of his company came back.

PART 1

CHAPTER 1:

A Day of Death, A Day of Birth

THE DAY WAS MARCH 8, 2008. I was with my daughter and her husband at Saint Mercy's Hospital in Sacramento, California. My daughter Anni was in labor, about to give birth to her second child, a baby girl. We'd been there all night. The labor was dragging out, going on 20 hours already.

My son-in-law Chris' phone rang and I could tell it was serious. After a few words were exchanged he handed it to me. That was strange. A call for me on his cell. It was Mary on the other line. She's the other grandmother of Anni's son, Jesse. She was at Anni's house, taking care of Jesse while his mom was in the hospital.

5

But this call had nothing to do with Jesse. This call was for me. Mary told me that military officers had just come to Anni's house, asking for us. She told them we were at the hospital, and though it was beyond their usual protocol, they were now on their way to the hospital to talk to us.

They wouldn't tell Mary anything more. She could only speculate. But she'd been through this kind of visit from the military before, in her family, and she knew what it meant. Mary also knew that Gabe was in the Army in Afghanistan. She knew this visit was going to be bad news and she called to warn us, to prepare us for what was to come.

The next several hours were a blur. The officers were on their way, maybe ten or twenty minutes from the hospital, but I couldn't wait to know what happened. I knew it would devastate me. I called them. I needed answers. But they refused to tell me anything until they could meet me in person.

As I was waiting, I called my oldest daughter, Heidi. She was already on her way to the hospital to be there with her sister. I didn't know what to say, maybe I shouldn't have called while she was driving. But I'd never done this before and I needed to tell her.

I had never announced a death before, nothing like this. I remember asking her to pull over to the side of the road. At least I thought of that. Then I told her what we knew. She was only five minutes away and she arrived at the hospital before the officers. I met her out front. She ran up to me. We held each other and cried.

Ten minutes later the officers showed up. They gave us a canned speech, I can't remember the words. It didn't really matter, he was dead.

The hospital chaplain heard what was happening and came to offer condolences. Nothing helps at a time like this, but her words felt compassionate, she offered help, but what could she do?

I was in shock. I couldn't think. I asked the officers to go give the news to Anni. I don't know why I thought that might be a good idea. I guess I thought it would be better coming from them. She screamed and yelled at them and made them leave her room.

What next? I needed to do something. My family would need to know. I went out into the hall and started calling close family members: my mom, my sisters, my brothers. I asked them to further pass the news. I couldn't do it.

Gabe's dad would need to know, even though he never knew Gabe and wasn't part of his life. Reynaldo and I hadn't talked in years. I don't think he even knew his son was a soldier. I had to call around his family just to track him down. We split and divorced when the girls were 2 and 3 and Gabe was just a baby. He hadn't been around when I was raising my kids and now he lived in Delaware.

When he answered the phone it surprised me that telling him was one of the hardest calls I made. I hadn't talked to him for so long, I couldn't even remember the last time. We weren't close, but it hurt so much to tell him that this child we created together was dead.

It was time for me to go back into the room. Anni was now very close to delivering her baby. She would have to give it all her attention. The only way she could do this was to put thoughts of her brother aside. I had to do the same.

Within an hour she was blessed with her healthy baby girl. They named her Jordan Lucy Enelia Watson *(Lucy after my mom, and Enelia after Anni's Aunt Nellie or Enelia)*. We were so relieved nothing had gone wrong. And Jordan was so sweet, she took our attention, at least for a while.

Yet, I was still hurting, just beginning to grasp Gabe's death. How I could lose my baby? How could I even go on? Anni had her baby, I had just lost mine. Every time I thought about it I'd start crying again.

It was getting hard for Anni to have us in the room. She didn't want our negative energy around her newborn. Anni's a strong, practical and smart woman and mother and she just couldn't deal with us being there.

We were all exhausted anyway, so we left. Heidi went home with her family. Mary took Jesse home to her house. I went to Anni's to sleep on her couch. I'd been staying with her while I was there.

My life had collapsed. Everyone else had gone separate directions and I was there, alone, with my sorrow.

CHAPTER 2:

Why Did Gabe Join the Army?

GABE ENLISTED IN 2003. We were living in Hornbrook, California, a run-down logging town near the Oregon border with maybe 200 inhabitants. I had bought a house there for cheap the year before, a fixer-upper. For me, living in the sticks was an adventure. For Gabe, I think it was his version of hell.

He'd just moved back in with me. We drove out, packed all his stuff in a trailer and brought him back from Utah. He had lived there with extended family the past year, staying in a house shared by my two brothers, their wives, and my mom. He was young and trying to get his life figured out.

Gabe had a daughter, Angela. She was only three years old at the time. She had Down Syndrome, but she knew her dad. He loved her and wanted to do his best for her. He decided to go to Utah when he split up with Angela's mom. He was struggling to find a way to support her.

I was happy when he decided to come back to California. But in Hornbrook he had nothing to do but sit in his room. He was bored. He didn't even try to find a job. He didn't have a car and the closest town was Yreka, still a small town of about 7,000. It was 15 miles away. There weren't a lot of options.

He decided to follow up on his Uncle Jason's advice to go into the Army. Jason was a veteran. He'd been in Operation Desert Storm, a war that was over within a month. Being in the Army helped Jason find his way to adulthood, and he suggested it might do the same for Gabe.

One day Gabe asked me to take him to Yreka where he met with recruiters. They were pretty convincing with the pretty pictures they painted. Within weeks he was signing the papers and shipping out.

I tried to talk him out of it. I don't like war and I didn't see any good reason for the US to be fighting in Iraq or Afghanistan.

I pleaded with him, "If you enlist now, you'll most likely have to fight."

"I know that, Mom. But I need to find a way to support Angela," he said.

"Yes, but if you die you won't even be here as part of her life. You won't be able to see her or take care of her," I replied.

We went round and round. But then he said, "I think I've always had a warrior spirit. I need to go to find out what that means to me, to find who I am."

I couldn't argue with that. The one thing I believe in most of all is living our true life, in integrity with our deepest, truest self. If this was what he felt called to do, there may have been other ways to express it, but I couldn't get in his way to stop it.

Still, I never liked him being there. I always struggled to make some kind of sense of it for myself. I knew he had to find his own way, but it was so hard to let him leave.

That last day, the recruiter came and picked him up. There was no pomp or ceremony. I was the only one home. They were taking Gabe to Portland for a week of shots and getting him ready. Then they'd fly him to Fort Sill in Oklahoma. I couldn't imagine what he was getting himself into. It tore at me deep inside. I was his mother and I wanted him home where he was safe.

CHAPTER 3:

The Funeral

THE DAYS FOLLOWING THE NEWS of Gabe's death were a jumble. To help navigate my numbness there were funeral arrangements and decisions to make. The ritual of the funeral gave me a needed focus at a time when I could have just crawled under a blanket and been lost to the world.

My sister, Lark, was tremendous support. I was needing something, pieces of Gabe I could grasp on to. Lark lived in Arizona, but we talked daily. She'd check in with me, send emails or calling. Lark owns a research business, she knows how to find things. She sent me news articles and other related links. Gabe's friends posted memorial videos, pictures and more.

I let my tears flow. I needed to feel it all. I hurt everywhere. I felt like a part of me had been torn from the very center of my being. I hurt as deeply as I loved.

That first day, after the shocking news, I started contacting Gabe's friends through a MySpace account that

Anni had set up for me. I had been living mostly in Mexico for the past year and she thought I should have an account so I could stay in touch with the family, especially Gabe. (MySpace was a social network that was still pretty popular back then, before Facebook was big.)

I felt an urgency to let everyone know. I went to Gabe's MySpace page and started inviting all of his friends to be my friends. Along with my friend invitation I shared the news of his death. Soon I had around a hundred new friends who were messaging me and offering their condolences. It felt good to connect with Gabe's friends. The stories gave me insights into the way he touched the lives of friends who knew and loved him.

We were contacted by a local TV station. They wanted to interview us. I resisted. I'm a private person and I didn't feel like it was anyone's business. But Anni thought we should give the interview. I never would have thought of publicity, but she helped me see that with the interview his death wouldn't go unseen.

There were articles in all the local papers, even in Yreka, CA, where he had enlisted. The last known address he had on file was from that area so he became one of their local heroes. He only lived there for a month or so before enlisting, yet when I go back there now I see they've posted his picture, along with others, in the County Courthouse and on the wall in the local grocery store. It brings me an odd mixture of pride, love and sadness.

There were so many decisions to make in those first few weeks after his death. None of us were in a great frame of mind for making them. Where would we even hold the funeral? The three of us were spread out. My girls were in California. Anni lived in Sacramento, Heidi had been living in the Central Valley, and I had been living in Mexico. None of these were places Gabe had ever called home.

We finally agreed on Concord, California, though we had moved away years before. If there was anywhere he would have called home, this was it. Concord was where Gabe went to school from about fourth grade through high school. He even attended Diablo Valley College for a few semesters. He still had close friends in Concord that he would visit with every time he came home on leave. Gabe's daughter and her mother, Amy, also lived there. So, it somehow made the most sense.

The military services helped us out more than I would have expected. Mary said they've come a long way since World War II and Vietnam. In those days the news would come in a telegram and there would be little other support. Sergeant Mendoza was assigned to our case. He walked us through every step of the way.

Mendoza met with us often. He explained the expenses that were covered. They had to fly Gabe's body back home. They covered his funeral, as could be expected, but there were some unexpected extras that helped make it easier. I had come to California for my granddaughter's birth and I already had my plane ticket back to Mexico for the following week. They extended my ticket to be there for the funeral and also paid for Reynaldo to fly in from Delaware for the service.

We decided on cremation. It was what we thought Gabe wanted. It was not a popular choice with some of our extended family or with his absentee father. But we were his family, me and his sisters, and even though Reynaldo had to sign off on it, he deferred to our decision.

We could have had him buried or placed his ashes at a military cemetery, or anywhere else we choose. But we weren't ready to part with him yet. For now he sits in an urn on my daughter's shelf.

Sgt. Mendoza was a regular in our lives for those few weeks. He helped us make decisions like finding the funeral home we would use, even driving us there to meet with them. I had never been through any of this before. I don't know what I would have done without him. He arranged to get Gabe's body flown home. On the day I went to meet the plane, he drove me to the airport and was there for moral support.

A part of me was in strong denial. I still couldn't accept that he was gone. I'm fairly intuitive and have a strong bond with my kids. I've known when my daughters were pregnant. I knew the name of my granddaughter, Angela, before her parents (Gabe and Amy) told me they'd decided on it.

I always felt my intuition would tell me if something bad happened to one of my kids, that's how it's supposed to work. But whether it was my refusal to believe that bad things could happen to me or some other block I had, I could not feel the reality that he was dead. I felt that somehow they had made a mistake. It seemed that someone should call us any day and set it straight. But, of course, that didn't happen.

So I needed to see his body and I was glad they were bringing him home. I needed the closure. I have a friend whose brother died in South America when he was young and they never found his body. He never got to see him again. He told me he's had a hard time with that all of his life.

I wanted even more connection to Gabe and his death. If I could have, I would have flown to Afghanistan myself. I wanted to touch the dirt where he died and see the barracks where he'd bunked. I needed to make it real, because for me, it still wasn't.

The day came for them to fly Gabe home. The weather was bad and they had to divert the plane from the Concord Airport to Napa, about half an hour away. Sgt. Mendoza picked me up and we drove to the Napa Airport. It was a small private airport. Gabe's friend, Sean, was there, and his sister, Kat. They were his close friends growing up. It rained. It felt like even the heavens were sad. Seeing the casket brought off the small plane, I cried and cried. It couldn't be real, it couldn't be his body inside. But obviously there was a body in the casket and I couldn't deny it any more.

We had a motorcycle procession all the way back from Napa to Concord. The Patriot Guard are a group of veterans that ride their motorcycles at military funerals, shielding families from those that would disrupt the services. They were there to lead the way. Their bikes were adorned with American flags, guiding us and stopping traffic along the route. I watched them out the window, the whole 30 miles back to Concord, arriving at the funeral home. It was quite a show. I felt like Gabe was smiling down from Heaven at the honor they were showing him. It took some of the edge off my pain.

The day of the funeral we had family coming in from everywhere. In addition to my mom and sisters, my youngest brother and nephews and nieces, we also had a big entourage from Reynaldo's side of the family, the Guzmans. People I hadn't seen in years arrived, from Gabe's dad to his aunts, uncles and cousins. Even a half-sister he never knew showed up. It felt good to see them and know they cared. Gabe's friends came out of the woodwork. His friends from school and childhood were there. Still more poured in ... some of the men who had become his comrades through trainings, being stationed together, and going on assignments ... they were there. Though the funeral parlor was big, with a capacity of a hundred or more, it couldn't fit them all.

The number of people who came surprised me. We were a small family. I was a single mother with my three kids. I had learned to be independent and I did most things by myself, just me and my kids. I didn't know that we even knew this many people.

We'd never settled in one area for very long. When my
kids were growing up I moved us around a lot, my
wandering spirit not letting me stay in one place. Gabe's
death was showing me how many lives he had touched.
Gabe had also been a bit of a loner. But he liked to hang out
with friends, he loved to joke around and laugh. Again, it
felt like Gabe was smiling down on us, even laughing,
happy to see all of his friends and family together. Through
the haze of my sadness, I felt the love.

It was here, at the funeral, I finally saw the open coffin. I
needed to spend some time with him. Yet, his body didn't
look like his. The face was different. I don't know if it was
because of the makeup or they just couldn't get his face to
look right. The reports were sketchy as to what really
happened to him. They just said 'blunt force trauma to the
head'. I would have liked a much more detailed description.
This one didn't sound lethal enough, how could it be true? I
read and checked the reports, but I couldn't find what I was
looking for. What was it I was looking for? It seemed far too
military-like that they couldn't give us all the facts. I wanted
the full story.

I wish I had spent more time with his body. I wish I'd
had some private time to just be with him. This body didn't
look like my son. But I had to accept the truth. Even though
he didn't look like Gabe, it was him. Even though I still wish
he could just walk through the door, all these years later, I
know he's gone.

Still, I wish I could go back and just be there with the
body of Gabe that was not really Gabe - how could he be

Gabe when the part that was truly him was gone and all that was left was a shell? I wish I could just stare at him longer, touch and feel him. But I was perhaps embarrassed or self-conscious that I shouldn't spend too much time there. Silly me, self-conscious at my own son's funeral. What did it matter who saw me or what they would think?

When the funeral service started I got up first to speak. I don't know how I did it. I didn't like speaking in front of people, but I knew I needed to, so I did. I wrote it out first and brought it with me. I knew I couldn't do it without notes. I somehow put words to my son's life. I gave my eulogy. It was a military funeral. The officers also shared. They told of Gabe's heroic moments. My brother had a turn, and a few others as well. Everyone's eyes were filled with tears.

They awarded Gabe's medals to me. He received the purple heart, the gold star, and several others. It felt so ironic that he had to die to be honored with these medals. Why does it take dying to be considered a hero? It is a status you get automatically when you are killed. He got about eight or more medals just for being dead. I didn't want the medals, I wanted my son!

As we finished up I stood at the front of the room and the people started to file out past me. We were heading outside for the 21-gun-salute. I hate guns, but the shots in his honor felt right. It felt like there couldn't be enough said or done to mark how special he was.

As the people walked past me, friends and family, each person took time to give me a hug and I blessed them and thanked them for coming. It was a mutual giving and receiving of love. We stood around afterwards, probably not really sure what to do, sharing greetings and awkward small talk. Amazing Grace was being played on bagpipes in front of the building. It's one of my favorite songs, one that seems so appropriate for funerals and memorials.

Within a week, our families had gone their separate ways and I was on a flight back to Mexico. This time I was taking with me the folded flag that had covered my son's coffin. I wasn't the same person who had arrived from Mexico a few weeks before.

CHAPTER 4:

When War Became Real for Me

I BEGAN TO LOVE AMAZING GRACE on the same trip where I saw firsthand the damages of war. It started on my first spiritual pilgrimage in October 2001 when I met an Irish bagpipe player named Sean Kelly.

It was a pilgrimage of peace and I joined spiritual author James Twyman on a trip to Europe, leaving just one month after 9/11. James (Jimmy) Twyman has been dubbed the "Peace Troubadour" after putting the peace prayers of the twelve major religions to music and playing them in concerts around the world.

I was new to this spiritual woo-woo stuff back then, and Jimmy was my first real teacher. I'd read Twyman's books, *"Emissary of Light"* and *"The Secret of the Beloved Disciple"*. I'd gone on a retreat he led in Joshua Tree, California, the previous year. I soaked up his material, wanting to emulate what he taught of love and connection and creating peace on our planet.

When this trip was announced I had just sold my condo in the Bay Area and had some spending money. At the time I had very little experience traveling outside of the US, but I was excited to go see these places and bring to life what I read about in Jimmy's books.

There were 60 people on this trip. I didn't know any of them before leaving home. We traveled to the places that Jimmy Twyman wrote about: Medjugorje in Bosnia/Herzegovina and Assisi, Italy.

The pilgrimage was a turning point in my life in many ways. I found compassion and understanding as we visited sacred sites, both in Bosnia and Italy. We were encouraged to "see as God sees" and I let go of judgments as I realized that God loves all of his people. I watched devotees climb the sacred Mt. Krizevac, demonstrating their love for God. I began to see people with new eyes.

Sean Kelly brought something special to the pilgrimage by bringing his bagpipes and full Scottish plaid and kilt. He pulled them out a few times ... once when we were leaving Medjugorje he played from the balcony. And when we arrived on a quiet night in Assisi, in a very playful mood, our group decided to do a musical parade and dance through the streets. My friend, Chuck, drummed on an upside down garbage can. Sean donned his full Scottish outfit and played his pipes as we marched along.

Yet, the most powerful time we saw Sean play was on the day we went to Mostar. It was a day that impacted us all; for me it was my first encounter with the effects of war.

Our group had spent several days in Medjugorje, a small valley town in Bosnia-Herzegovina with a population of 2,300. The town has a long-standing spiritual history. In 1933, commemorating the 1900th year since the death of Jesus, the village built a cross on their highest mountain, Mt Krizevac. The 16-ton cross contains a relic of the True Cross, received from Pope Pius XI in Rome. The path up the mountain soon became a pilgrimage for people who would travel from far away lands to climb the sacred mountain, passing the stations of the cross along the way.

Medjugorje gained more fame in 1981, when six local children claimed they had seen visions of the Virgin Mary, which continued even as they grew into adulthood. They would be visited daily and receive messages from the Virgin Mother. These six children became known as the *"visionaries"*, sharing their messages from Mary with all that would listen. The town blossomed into a major pilgrimage destination for Catholics and others, something which continues to this day.

Medjugorje was our first destination and our first stop was to see the "visionary", one of the original six. The others had gone on with their lives, but this one continued to receive and share a daily message from Mother Mary.

Her message that day, October 25, 2001, said:

"Dear children! Also today I call to you to pray from your whole heart and to love each other. Little children, you are chosen to witness peace and joy. If there is no peace, pray and you will receive it. Through you and your prayer, little children, peace will begin to flow through the world. That is why, little children, pray, pray, pray, because prayer works miracles in human hearts and in the world. I am with you and I thank God for each of you who has accepted and lives prayer with seriousness. Thank you for having responded to my call."

The message had a catholic slant, but I looked past the religion and felt the love spoken in the words. I prayed for peace in the way that Jimmy taught, seeing that our desire for peace and love goes past all religion, it is universal.

We had free time and each of the four days we were there, I climbed Mt Krizevac. Our group went up together on our final day. We shared stories of peace. Later I learned that Medjugorje had not been touched by the Bosnian War. In fact, there were stories of bombs being dropped, but by some divine intervention they did not land. It's hard to say whether this was true, but either way, Medjugorje was spared the effects of the war.

One day our group went to Mostar, less than 30 miles away, and we saw an entirely different side of things. Mostar is a picturesque little town that sits in a valley with a river flowing through the middle. A bridge spans the river, connecting the two sides of the city, one side being Catholic and the other being Muslim.

We started the day visiting the newly rebuilt Catholic cathedral. The cathedral had been destroyed in the war and so far they had only constructed a large concrete shell. This was the third time, over centuries of wars, that the cathedral was rebuilt. The priest told stories of the more recent Bosnian War of the 90's. He told of the destruction of the cathedral and the bridge, both icons of the town. The cathedral had been bombed and the Madonna was inside. Miraculously, a young priest carried the heavy statue out. I'd read some other stories before the trip. They told of neighbors and friends turning on each other and forcing them out of their homes.

Walking through town I saw buildings that were torn apart and riddled with bullet holes. Growing up in the USA I was buffered all my life from these kind of scenes. The effects of war always seemed far away, they happened to someone else. Now I was seeing what war looked like, yet I knew that even on this journey I only got a glimpse of understanding of what these people had been through. This was just the aftermath and I was only seeing the ruined buildings. What I didn't see, couldn't see, but could only get a sense of, were the effects of war on the people.

We walked across a suspended footbridge to the Muslim side of town. They were still rebuilding the "Old Bridge" that the city was known for. This was the only way to cross. Even after the war, the two sides of the city were interconnected. The small bridge was crowded with people going back and forth.

On the Muslim side I felt like I was in a different world. We came to a market where they sold shiny copper plates, painted and lacquered by hand. We passed rows of shops, all with handmade local crafts. We had come to visit the mosque, the symbol of religion for these people. It was a beautiful building with elaborate decoration. It was the first time I'd ever been in a mosque. As we entered we had to leave our shoes at the door and cover our heads. We stayed for the service.

This trip had focused on Mother Mary and Saint Francis. Both had promoted peace. Saint Francis had taught that war should not be fought over religious ideas. But this town had lived through those kind of wars, many times over. I wasn't Catholic or Muslim, but everyone had been kind to us on both sides of the river. People were basically the same. I was so sad to see the destruction of their lives.

As we came out of the mosque, a white dove flew in front of us. We were quiet. No one felt much like talking. Everyone knows that doves are a symbol of peace. It felt like it was there for us.

We returned over the bridge and walked back to the Catholic Cathedral to end the day. We sat in the cathedral and took turns sharing our thoughts and feelings. Dione, one of the older ladies, played her violin for us. Then Sean stood up. I didn't know he had the bagpipes with him. He played Amazing Grace. All the feelings of the day burst through me with the song and I couldn't stop crying.

CHAPTER 5:

Tezcatlipoca,

The Lord of Destruction

WHEN I CAME TO MEXICO IN 2006, two years before Gabe died, I never thought of living there. I planned to spend six months to research and learn about the area so I could make connections and organize my spiritual tours. My first visit was a few years before, only for ten days, but I felt such a deep connection to the land, I wanted to go back. I was drawn to the beauty and friendly people, to their simple and natural way of life.

But a few months after I arrived in Tepoztlán I got involved with a man, Roberto, who had a retreat center in Amatlán. He invited me to live with him and help out. By then I was enchanted with the warm climate and the semitropical jungle, where everything about life was so different. I'd already quit my job in the US and with nothing to really go back to, it was easy to say yes.

Roberto was a bit of a scholar on the Mayan Calendar. He told me about the Tzolkin and how to calculate my Mayan Day Sign. He explained how the sacred calendar, that was actually used by the Mayan people and had been around for thousands of years, was not the same as what the New Age author José Argüelles taught. It was much more complex. It described life on Earth since its inception.

In the Mayan Calendar, the year of November 18, 2007 to November 12, 2008, was known as the 5th Night, ruled by the energy of Tezcatlipoca, the Mesoamerican God of Darkness or Lord of Destruction. These legends of the Mayan Calendar sounded like some made up fantasy novel, but as I began to understand it, it started making more sense.

I read a book titled *"Solving the Greatest Mystery of our Time: The Mayan Calendar"* by Carl Calleman *. In it, Calleman describes the long count, a system that goes back to the creation of the Universe, and shows how the different periods tie in with historical evidence. He also compares the Mayan Calendar to other calendar systems from the Egyptians to the Bible. He shows how the Mayan Calendar is physically displayed in the ancient pyramids. The mathematical equations are complex and precise.

In my studies, I had learned that Tezcatlipoca brought some hard times. Historically, the periods when

Tezcatlipoca has ruled the heavens have been some of the worst destruction known on our planet. The way the Long Count of the Mayan Calendar works, the first cycle began with a period of 63 million-plus years, the intervals getting 20 times shorter each time they came around, like the steps of a pyramid, each cycle building on the broader cycle below. In these cycles there are days and nights, with a different God ruling the energy of each day and each night. As you can imagine, the nights were the periods of dark and shadow, followed by the enlightenment of day. But the 5th night was the worst.

As Calleman explains, Tezcatlipoca was ruling during a 40-year period that saw the rise of Hitler and then brought us into World War II. Tezcatlipoca ruled during years of the Dark Ages and the Inquisition, another period of mass genocide. He ruled during the Ice Age, when much of the animal and plant life was wiped out.

This 360-day period during 2007-2008 coincided with the financial crisis that hit our nations, causing thousands of people to lose their jobs and homes. On a personal scale, I met so many people that year that had difficult and life-changing catastrophes. I still meet people who tell me about death, loss of a job or other difficulties and when I ask when it happened it was in 2008.

Tezcatlipoca is no minor God. In the Aztec pantheon Quetzalcoatl is the God of enlightenment. Tezcatlipoca is his enemy and destroyer. He is known to bring chaos.

I don't base my life on ancient gods and goddesses, but I do believe the way they're described relates to something real in the cosmic forces. So I look at what they represent. Something was definitely happening in 2008, not just because the Mayan Calendar said it would, not just something that was happening to someone else out there in the world, but destruction was happening in my life and in the lives of people I knew and met.

I was only beginning to understand it. When this period started and Roberto told me about it, I brushed it aside and didn't really think much of it. How bad could it be? But in 2008 I started realizing how its predictions were showing up in my life. The death of my son was the beginning of a really bad year for me. I still had no idea what Tezcatlipoca had in store.

Carl Calleman is a leading scholar dedicated to understanding the ancient Mayan calendar and its underlying mechanisms and making this understandable to modern people. For further reading, visit: Calleman.com

CHAPTER 6:

Life Back In Mexico

AFTER THE FUNERAL, I returned to Mexico a wreck, walking like a zombie through my days. But I had to pull myself together for my work. I had delayed my return for the funeral, but I needed to be there to help manage the retreat center where I lived. Roberto had previous plans to go to Argentina for five weeks, leaving me in charge.

The work wasn't demanding, mostly greeting the guests and organizing what they needed. I enjoyed the people who showed up. It was a nice, much needed distraction.

The place had a magical quality that drew people in. They would come from all over the world, though most were Mexicans coming from Mexico City, just an hour and a half to the north.

They would come to our retreat center in the mountains for a spiritual renewal. We'd get shamanic and yoga groups, as well as individuals, couples and vagabond travelers. The retreat center was at the end of a bumpy dirt road, at the mouth of a canyon. It wasn't easy to get to. We'd never advertise, but people would hear about us from others and find their way there. Everyone was welcome. Some would come for a visit, just for a walk through or to enjoy a picnic in the gardens. The groups usually came with plans and reservations.

We provided sleeping accommodations for up to 40 people when all the beds were full. We were satisfied with about half that many. Syncronicities happened when I was there. I've always experienced Mexico as a magical place and the retreat center was extra special.

When I was left in charge, that magical energy drew people in like a magnet. As soon as Roberto left the people started arriving. I found this to be true every time I was I was put in charge while he was away. It wasn't that we didn't have guests when he was there. We did. And the guests liked Roberto a lot. He was seen as kind of a shaman and people would come asking to hear his wisdom. His accommodation rates were low and his heart was open. Business always had a steady flow. Yet I'd always notice that as soon as he was gone we'd get immediately busier.

I was back a week when Roberto left for Argentina for his daughter's wedding. That day two guys from Los Angeles came in a van. They stayed for four days. Then a couple from Mexico City came for a night or two. It was a steady trickle the whole time he was gone. The weekends would fill up with groups ranging from 20 to 30 people. One weekend I had seven separate groups; people were there from Friday through Sunday. We ran two sweat lodge ceremonies that weekend. And the separate groups had their own schedules and activities going on the entire time. It was enough for our housekeeper to almost pull her hair out.

Running the place was pretty easy. We would serve meals for the big groups. Our lead housekeeper would plan the meals and make shopping lists. I would drive Roberto's van to the markets in town and fill it up with the supplies we needed. Some groups wanted a sweat lodge (called a temescal) which also meant we had to prepare the lodge and cover it with blankets, build the sacred fire and lead the ceremony. Roberto usually led the ceremony, but he had arrangements for someone to stand in when he was gone. My part was arranging everything, making bookings, greeting guests and keeping things running smoothly.

In many ways the work was good for me and kept me busy. But in my quiet time, when I was alone, I would go up to my bed and lay there, playing "My Angel Gabriel" over and over on my CD player. It was a song that Gabe liked (for obvious reasons) and one the family had chosen to play at the funeral. I would just lay there and listen to it, hitting play each time it ended, to hear it again. I missed him so much.

CHAPTER 7:

Meeting Someone New

TWO WEEKS HAD PASSED. It was the middle of the week and I was doing my usual thing, laying on the couch listening to Gabe's song. That's how I thought of it. Gabe was an angel now, he was my angel Gabriel.

I was staying in Roberto's house while he was gone. We called it the Tree House, not because it was built in a tree, but because it surrounded a tree. There was a Ciruelo, or Chinese Plum, growing up through the middle of the house, branching out above, covered with leaves and shade in the rainy season. It was just a simple jungle hut, built of wood, 20 feet up a small hill, against the cliff.

I could look down and see the eight tipis below. The rainy season was approaching and the plum, lime and banana trees were coming into bloom. The leaves made it difficult to see what was going on in the garden, but it was a sweet view.

I thought I heard a noise so I turned off my music and went down to see if anyone was there. I found two men looking around.

I introduced myself, "Soy Ixchel." (*I am Ixchel.*) This is the spiritual name I'd been given by Roberto shortly after moving there and I used it with everyone.

The first man introduced himself, in English, as Mark. His friend was Chez.

"We wanted to see La Puerta *(the door)*." He said. "We live in the area but haven't been here before."

I thought Mark was cute and sexy. He had broad shoulders and strong muscles, short brown hair and a dimple on his chin. His friend, Chez, was a funny looking man, older with wild unruly hair. But Mark had a sly humor that played with Chez' oddness.

I showed them *"La Puerta"*, a large natural arch carved into the tall cliff face.

I explained: "It's considered an interdimensional doorway. Some people think that *'the door'* opens once a year and you can go through. Or if you meditate on it long enough, it will open.

"The story is that Quetzalcoatl, who was born in Amatlán, was at the doorway watching ants going back and forth, carrying seeds on their backs. He asked them what they were doing. They taught him to shrink down to their size, which he did, and he followed them through. Then he brought back to the people the seeds for corn and beans."

I said, "Personally, I like what Roberto says the best. He tells people 'whatever is outside is inside, when you open your heart you open all the doors'."

Then I showed them the *"heart of the puerta"*. It was formed by the long roots of the amate tree that grew down the cliff. The roots had formed what looked like a heart on the rock face. I continued showing Mark and Chez around so they could see the inside of the tipis, each with 4-5 beds, the outdoor kitchen that looks out over the river and fields on the other side of the road and the large palapa we used as a dining area. I even showed them the compost toilets and showers. I topped it off as we circled back to the round-shaped meditation hut and the sweat lodge area.

We returned to sit in the garden. I wanted to spend more time with Mark.

He spoke good English, but with an accent. He looked European. "Where are you from?" I asked.

"We're both Polish" he said, "but we didn't know each other before coming to Mexico. Even though I've been here several years, I just recently met Chez."

We talked for a while. I knew Mark was younger than me, maybe by ten years or so, still I was instantly attracted. I'd been single for a while; Roberto and I had split up in October, and were just friends and business partners now. But it was more than just attraction. We were drawn to each other, and I needed someone.

39

The next day Mark came back alone, just to see me. We talked and got to know each other better. I thought he was older than he was, but learned he was 34. He thought I was younger, I was 49. It didn't stop us from wanting to spend time together.

I told him about Gabe. He asked if my feelings for him were because I was trying to replace my son. I didn't think they were. He wasn't like Gabe, other than their dry and sarcastic humor. But hanging out with him felt good, in a way that was similar to hanging out with my kids. My kids are some of my favorite people to be with, just relaxing and fun together. For whatever reason, I liked him.

Mark came by often. When I could get away we'd go for a walk. Or we'd just hang out at the tipis and sometimes watch a movie. He helped me out with all kinds of things from lugging a heavy tipi to translating for a bilingual retreat I was leading. He'd come by on weekends and help me with the groups. Sometimes he'd stay for the temezcal (sweat lodge ceremony). He was drawn to the ceremony.

I found out he had a girlfriend. He told me they weren't getting along. They lived together. She had a baby girl, not his, but they'd been together for a while and he was the only dad the baby knew. He said he wasn't really "together" with his girlfriend, but he had a strong sense of responsibility and he couldn't just leave.

I knew it wasn't fair to her, but I needed a man in my life. He filled a hole in me. His friendship and support helped me heal. I wasn't ready to push that away. I kept seeing him.

CHAPTER 8:

Getting Away for a Day

BY MID-MAY I'D SETTLED BACK INTO THE LIFE of
running the retreat center. The hardest part for me was
feeling I needed to be there all the time. I don't like being so
tied down. I couldn't get away for even a walk in the
mountains. When I went to town I'd hurry and buy what I
needed and rush back, not taking time to say "Hi" to friends
or even for a visit at the coffee shop.

I talked to Roberto on the phone and told him how I felt.
He said I should just lock things up or leave our cleaning
lady in charge and go when I needed to go. We weren't busy
all the time. I still didn't feel comfortable leaving. The place
was remote, and even though it had a 7' to 8' stone fence
around it, it didn't feel right to leave it unattended. Someone
needed to be there to greet visitors and guests.

One day a man showed up on a motorcycle asking to see Roberto about his jewelry. Roberto had a side business selling necklaces, pendants, and bracelets with replicas of the ancient Aztec, Olmec and Mayan jewelry that had been found in the pyramids and archaeological sites. It was beautiful, handcrafted work made of jade, turquoise and other semi-precious stones.

I told the man that Roberto wasn't there, but he wanted to just hang out. I didn't like his vibe, but it wasn't unusual for people to hang around, so I didn't know what else to say.

It was early afternoon and I needed to go into town for some shopping. Getting to town and back usually took a couple of hours and if I didn't leave soon it would be too late. In Mexico we live by the sun. The market closes around 4:00 to 5:00 pm.

Remembering what Roberto had said, that sometimes I needed to just go and not let the place become a prison, I figured I should go get the shopping done.

I started getting ready to leave, but the visitor was still there and I found him in the garden, talking to a guest we had. The guest was a nice, friendly man who had been staying a few days. Our guest said he wasn't going anywhere, so I asked if he could lock up if he did decide to leave. I didn't feel good about the visitor, but I didn't have any reason to think badly of him. So I left them together and went into town.

On my way back, about a mile from home, I noticed the visitor driving away on his motorcycle. I was tired. I passed and continued on my way back.

I drove home and unloaded the groceries. No one else was there. Then I went up to the house. As I walked in the first thing I saw was the desk and I noticed that my computer was gone. It didn't make sense. I stood there dumbly, not knowing what to do. It slowly sank in that we'd been robbed.

Panic started setting in. I began searching the place to see what else was missing. My printer was gone. And my digital camera, though he missed the camera's battery charger. My backpack, for carrying my computer, was sitting there next to the desk. Funny he didn't think of using it.

I had a stash of money in my backpack. It was untouched. But the phone had been ripped out of the wall. I guess he didn't want us calling for help. Obviously he'd been in a hurry and just grabbed what was easy and accessible.

If I hadn't known a computer should have been sitting on the desk I wouldn't have even noticed anyone had been there. There was no mess or anything. Not like you see in the movies. He'd just helped himself to whatever he could take that was valuable.

I sat down and cried. My computer had been new, I'd just bought it on this last trip to the US. The trip I was on when Gabe died.

I relied on my computer for everything. I used it for my work building websites. The help I gave at the retreat center didn't bring much money and I needed this as a supplement. All my files, all of my website work, and everything I had was on my computer.

My pictures were on it, too, including pictures of the family. Pictures of Gabe felt more precious than ever and many of those were on the computer. There were pictures of his last visit home and pictures of the funeral. I was the only one who had pictures from the day he was brought off the airplane. I was devastated. I shook with the tears and the feeling of betrayal. I'd never experienced a robbery like this before and it cut deep to my core. I felt like I was torn open and vulnerable.

I thought back to seeing him on the road. He had been making his getaway. If only I'd known. But what would I have done? What could I have done?

More importantly, what should I do now? He couldn't be too far away. But could anyone find or catch him?

At first I thought Roberto had gotten off easy, that the robber hadn't taken much that was his. I could see his necklaces still draped on hooks around the house. There was a glass table in front of the sofa that was kind of like an altar, covered with some of Roberto's favorite stones. The table was untouched.

Roberto had a suitcase lying on the floor. He had brought it back from the gem show in Tucson. He'd left it there, filled with his newer work and the jewelry he had for sale. It was still lying there, untouched. Then I got thinking about it. The zipper had been left unzipped. It still looked the way it had, but I hadn't checked inside.

I opened it. It was empty. He had taken all of Roberto's newer work, every last piece. It was thousands of dollars worth of jewelry.

I knew I'd have to break the news to Roberto that we'd been robbed and that it was partly my fault. I dreaded telling him, but I knew it was better to tell him while he was still in Argentina and give him time to process his feelings. It would be much better than hitting him with the news a few weeks later, when he got home. Better for him and better for me.

I had to find a phone. We had an old phone to plug into the wall when the power went out. I dug it out, plugged it in.

Still trembling, I called Roberto. I needed his advice. I didn't know what to do about something like this. Call the *policia*? Or local friends? What happens when you get robbed in Mexico?

True to his nature, Roberto was understanding and forgiving. He wasn't upset with me, just upset about the robbery. I always learned a lot from him, he knew how to let go of things that were beyond his control and not turn them into blame and painful drama.

He had me call his business partner. He said the police would do nothing and it's best not to let the news out, around the town. People will take advantage if they see you as vulnerable. There was nothing we could really do.

The days following the robbery I had a lot of time to think. Without my computer to work with, I had a very quiet break from the world of the internet. The cyber world has it's way of sucking me in and occupying my time.

Perhaps that was part of the lesson for me, or at least something positive I could take away from the experience. Maybe I could find more balance with my work and spend more time with myself. I could get out in nature, though I was more afraid than ever to leave the place unattended.

I've been a workaholic ever since I was a young adult and my mom was my boss. I worked as an independent insurance auditor, my former career that had supported me and my kids for over 20 years. The benefit of being self-employed is the flexibility, but the flip side of working from home is that the work time can carry over into all areas of my life. I have a hard finding balance and it's been one of my biggest struggles.

With my computer gone, I now had empty time in my day. Mark came by at times to offer support. And I still had business to take care of. But I had a lot of time alone. I went out and sat in the garden in the mornings. I contemplated my life. I tend to look at my life as a witness to myself. I ask myself why I attract the experiences I've had. My belief is that our soul guides us to live from our deeper truth and to discover our true essence. We are so much more than our bodies and our personalities. This inner search has revealed more than I ever would have thought. I've found in it that I really like being me.

But I wasn't quite that far along when I was processing the fresh grief of my son's death and feeling the impact of just being robbed. I was asking myself what the heck was going on. I was full of questions: *Why did I have to experience so much in such a short time? Was I just unlucky or stupid? Was I a bit too naive to think that bad things didn't or couldn't happen to me because I'm basically a good person?*

Contemplating what I could learn from the experience, it was obvious to me that I'd ignored my intuition. I hadn't been paying enough attention. My gut told me this guy was bad, but without my rational mind having a reason to suspect him, I let it pass.

I felt there was more to it, something for me to learn that was deeper than these obvious lessons. In the crazy aftermath of death and robbery, I kept searching for meaning. Not everything has to make sense, but I felt there were some lessons for me to embrace so I could grow.

My son's death was an awful thing, but in accepting it for what it was perhaps there was a way to move through the pain. I loved him so much. I never want the feeling of love and connection with my son to go away.

It felt like a deeper transformation was occurring in me. Powerful change comes from powerful experiences. I felt like a caterpillar getting ready to be a butterfly. When the caterpillar goes into a cocoon its body dissolves entirely and from the imaginal cells it creates the new body of the butterfly. It is no longer the same caterpillar. It is truly a new being. My transformation was breaking me down like this, dissolving all that I thought I was.

I meditated in the garden. It was there that I remembered that this was the year of Tezcatlipoca. I hadn't put it together until then, when two terrible things happened in a row. It was becoming easier to see destructive forces in my life.

When I first heard the predictions of what the year of Tezcatlipoca's rule would bring I never thought it applied to me, at least not so personally. Now it seemed I was living it out. I was going through the chaos that Tezcatlipoca brings.

So I thought about it more. What did Tezcatlipoca represent and why did I need this breaking down and chaos? Could I rise from the ashes?

Had I not seen lessons I needed to learn? And couldn't there be an easier way. Maybe I'd been too complacent and ignoring things that weren't working for me. Maybe I'd been letting things gradually get worse and worse, like a frog being cooked alive in hot water. Was I getting metaphorically 'cooked alive', not realizing it was time to jump out? Did I need this big push? What was it all pushing me to see or do?

I went back to Calleman's books. He wrote specifically about this time known as *"The Fifth Night"*:

"Creativity is born out of chaos and if you think more deeply about it you realize that there is no linear way from today's world (2004) to the Enlightened (2011). Instead the enlightened world can only emerge out of a series of transformative pulses, including periods of destruction, such as the Fifth NIGHT.

"The paradox to understand is that the very process that seems to break down the world economy and political dominance is also the one that paves the way for Enlightenment. The emergence of a fully enlightened collective state of consciousness can only thrive in a global consciousness that is balanced. This is because the imbalance that has been dominating humanity for some 5000 years has had as its direct cause the dualist frame of consciousness that was ruling throughout this time."

How could I apply this to my situation? What could I learn? Was there anything that would help me through? I wanted these crazy things to stop. I wanted to get the lesson and for my life to get better again.

There were other ways to look at Tezcatlipoca. I'd read in a book by Don Miguel Ruiz, author of *"The Four Agreements"*, that Tezcatlipoca also represents the *"smoking mirror"*. He teaches us to see through the illusions of the material world, to look past the illusion to what is real. This is like the wizard in *"The Wizard of Oz"*. Rather than the illusion of the *"mighty and powerful Oz"* we look behind the curtain and he is just an ordinary man.

I started looking at my situation and my relationships with the world and everyone around me through a different lens. What was the illusion and what was real?

When it came to my son, he was dead, but my love was still real. It was deep and powerful and I felt it to the core of my being. I know he loved me and I loved him. That love never dies. I held onto the belief that relationships and love are what matter.

The experience with the robber had taught me something quite different. All I had to do was look past the illusions of my mind to know what my gut was telling me. I knew he wasn't safe. Being robbed had instilled fear in me, a vulnerability. After the robbery I found it even harder to leave the house and retreat center. But my intuition had guided me. I could trust it. I just needed to remember to pay attention and act on my hunches. I was better safe than sorry.

As far as the things that were stolen, I knew that the material things didn't matter so much. They were just stuff and they could be replaced. It was definitely inconvenient. I didn't have the money for another computer.

I took this time to look at my relationship to possessions in a different way. I wanted to find a better balance to my work and spend less time at my computer. It seemed like the computer had just become another chain that kept me shackled and stuck.

In fact, being robbed also made me stretch out of my independent nature and ask others for help. I didn't have the money to replace my computer so some of my clients tried to get one donated. My daughter came through for me and bought me a new one. I'd always felt so alone, but I started to realize I had friends and support all around me. I had learned from Roberto about letting go and this year was a big one for me to put that into practice. Not letting go of love, but of stuff.

I put more value on friends and family. The time I spent with them was precious time that could not be regained. I opened my heart and let people in. I felt a sense of being different. I had transformed. I wasn't the same person I was before all this happened.

But just to be sure, I got tested again, a couple of months later. They say bad things often happen in threes. I certainly got my dose of it this year!

CHAPTER 9:

It Was a Dark and Stormy Night

BY JULY we were in the middle of the rainy season and this year was extra wet. Roberto had returned so I had a lot more free time. Mark and I would take walks in the canyons or splash around in waterfalls. The rivers were full and everything turned green.

Mark had arrived in the afternoon we'd gone for a walk, but then it got late, too late to take a combi (the public minibuses) and it had started to rain. He didn't have a way to get home so I let him borrow my car.

The car wasn't running very well. The transmission had broken down when I first brought it to Mexico and although it had been fixed it never really ran right after that. The last few times I drove it, it seemed to be getting worse. But it was good enough to keep him dry and get him home in the rain.

He didn't bring it back the next day. That night the rains came even harder. It was one of those torrential tropical rains. I'd gone to bed, but then the phone rang and woke me up.

It was Mark. It was hard to hear him or make out what he was saying. We had a bad connection. But I could tell he was upset.

I finally pieced it together. He'd been run off the road by some lunatics that were after him and his girlfriend and trying to kill them. They were up on the autopista (highway) and they had crashed into the woods. He'd been driving my car.

It was a crazy night. I was miles away. I couldn't help. I stayed on the phone with him for a while.

He had to get away from the car, something about the guys that ran him down and the cops. He didn't know where to go. He knew he needed to hide from the guys. He didn't want to go near the highway.

The night was black. Rain was pouring down everywhere.

His arm was hurt, but he said he could move.

Then we lost phone connection. I tried calling, but couldn't get him back. I tried to get back to sleep.

Around three in the morning Mark knocked on my door. He'd walked about five miles in the rain to get there. He was dripping wet and in pain. He thought his arm might be broken. I let him in and dried him off. Eventually we fell asleep.

The next morning we had to track down his girlfriend and make sure she was okay. She'd had her year-and-a-half-old daughter with her in the car. They had gone separate ways after the crash, trying to keep the bad guys from finding them. We found they had made it home to safety as well.

His girlfriend had a broken finger, but that was all, and her daughter was unscathed. It felt like a miracle that the three of them were even alive.

We needed to get Mark's arm looked at. Amatlán was just a small pueblo, several miles east of Tepoztlán, the nearest town. Both towns are severely lacking in hospitals. Roberto drove us to the medical center in Tepoztlán, but then dropped us off.

The medical center said they couldn't do anything until Mark got an X-ray. We were sent to a radiology office a half mile away for that. A couple hours later we were back. By then we knew it was broken, but they had to confirm it before they sent us off again, this time to the hospital in Cuernavaca, about an hour away by car. They couldn't set the broken bone there in Tepoztlán.

We took a bus and arrived at the hospital. It was early afternoon and started raining again. Roads were flooding. We jumped across gutters flowing with six-inch-deep water and rushed inside.

At the hospital we were instructed to stand in a crowded hallway and wait. We leaned against the wall for several hours. Our wet clothes had time to dry. When they finally called Mark they took a minute to look at the X-rays and said they would have to admit him. They would put him in a bed where he would have to wait a week before they could operate and fix his arm. And, no, he couldn't just come back a week later. He'd lose his place in the queue.

I couldn't believe it! In the States they would just set it right there on the spot. A regular doctor could have done it. Here it would take them a week for a simple broken bone. And of course by then they would have no option but to operate.

After a long day we simply left. Tired and dejected, we stepped back into another burst of rain and caught the bus back home. Mark said he'd figure something else out. The next day he found a *huesero,* a medicine man that specializes in healing bones. He got it fixed the old-fashioned way.

We weren't done. We had to track down the car. We discovered that it was towed. Finding it was another adventure, typical of Mexico. No one seemed to know where it was. We were sent to a tow yard on the south end of Cuernavaca only to be sent another hour south to some pit stop off the highway.

I don't know how we found the place, but we could tell we were in the right place by the field of junk cars. It was in the middle of nowhere. Nothing around. There was a small concrete block house with a woman and her kids out in the yard. We asked her about my car.

She found her husband for us and we told him what we were looking for. We didn't know what to expect. Mark hadn't had much chance to assess the damage the night of the crash. But my hopes weren't high.

When we found the car, amidst the other wrecked cars, it was pretty awful. I could see what a miracle it was Mark and his family had survived. The front end was bashed in, the sides were all scraped up, the tires couldn't even turn. It was totaled.

We stayed long enough to gather what belongings we could. I couldn't remember what was in it beforehand, but it was obvious someone had helped themselves to some of it.

Yet, none of that mattered much. There wasn't much that could be salvaged.

We made arrangements to sell it to the tow company for the value of the tires and salvageable parts. It offset the bill they wanted us to pay for having towed it. Not too different from the States in that way. If there was any money leftover, it was negligible.

By the time things calmed down, a few weeks later, I realized how much I had changed through all these experiences. I'd gone through one crisis after another. And this one could have been so much worse.

Along the way I had learned to truly let go. It wasn't that I was giving up. I was just learning to see through the world of illusion and material possessions and past them to what truly held meaning.

When the car was wrecked it surprised me how easy it was to kiss it goodbye. It seemed so unimportant to me. It just didn't matter.

What did matter were the miracles that played out through it all. What mattered was that Mark, his girlfriend, and her young daughter walked away with only minor injuries. It felt that angels had been watching over us the whole time and I think my Angel Gabriel was one of them.

PART 2

CHAPTER 10:

Making Sense of It All

SEPTEMBER CAME AND I WAS ON MY WAY BACK to California again. It was time to reconnect with my girls. We hadn't seen each other since right after the funeral. Our lives had changed, each of us finding our way through the grief.

On the flight home I had time to reflect. I was still trying to make sense of Gabe's death. What did it all mean to me? How was I to move forward? We were different. I was a peacemaker, Gabe chose the army. Even though it would never be my choice, I wanted to understand why he would choose army life.

When he'd left for basic training, I was attending local Toastmasters meetings. I had been part of this group for several months. I was a shy kid growing up and all through school and had quite successfully avoided public speaking.

But I was trying to put myself out in the world more. I needed to push myself and learn to give an engaging, or at least interesting, public presentation.

One of our meetings stands out in my memory because of the speeches made. They made an impact on me. And they helped me sort out some of my feelings about the Army.

There were two speeches given that day by a lady named Karen. Yet these two stories were opposite in the parable or lesson you would take from them. I like to see both sides of the coin so I paid attention, perhaps even more so because they were delivered by the same lady and on the same day.

Karen's first speech was when she got picked for a two-minute impromptu speech. She told us of her experience the week before when she was helping out at her granddaughter's kindergarten class and they had a fire drill. It was during nap time and the kids were resting. Their shoes and coats were lined up by the door. The kids were laying on their mats.

When the fire drill rang the kids quickly did as they were told and got in line and filed out the door to their designated spot. But there was one little girl that insisted on putting on her shoes. She had just learned to tie her shoes, by herself, and she had to do it herself. She carefully tied the bow, trying to get it just right. Karen was urging her to move or to let her do it, but she couldn't budge this stubborn little girl who wanted to put on her own shoes.

The point of her speech was, of course, that *"if this had been an actual emergency ..."* it would be folly to take the time to slow down, even to put on shoes. Perhaps one might grab shoes and a jacket on the way out, but first priority is to get out and away from the burning building. Following orders here is important!

Her conclusion in this speech was that there are times that we should act without thinking. We should just respond or obey the order, such as the siren of the fire drill.

Later she got up for her second speech. This was Karen's prepared five-minute speech.

It was a history lesson. Karen and her husband had a hobby of going with a local group in Northern California that retraced the trails of the old soldiers and wagon trains. They would look for lost buttons from uniforms and other memorabilia.

On this occasion she told of their group crossing paths with a history teacher that was taking his middle-school class on a re-enactment of a wagon train. This teacher taught by action and experience. He had the students make their own clothes, cook their own meals, and live the life of the wagon train for a few days.

That night the two groups built a fire and sat together, sharing stories. The teacher told of his classes and his hands-on methods. He explained how he taught the kids about Hitler. The kids said they couldn't understand how an entire country would allow themselves to be led by a monster such as Hitler. Trying to explain to the kids how people go along with the crowd didn't seem to help. How could anyone go along with the atrocities of a man like Hitler? Certainly none of them could imagine ever doing that!

The class needed an experiential lesson. With no explanation or preamble, the teacher took the class down the hall and led them into a windowless and dark room.

All the lights were turned off.

The students didn't know what was going on or why they were there. After a minute or so they began to fidget.

The teacher just stood there, not saying anything.

A few more minutes went by. They were getting more restless.

Finally, one of the kids said, "What are we doing? When are we getting out of here?"

The teacher took this as his cue. He turned on the lights and said, "You could have left five minutes ago. No one was stopping you. The door wasn't locked."

Of course the kids had not thought of questioning their teacher. He explained that this is how people follow along with the crowd. There is an unspoken social pressure to do what the group is doing and to go along with the person in charge, even when they lead you into a dark room or into danger.

The lesson was obvious. How often do we follow blindly? Or go along with our friends or a bigger group? When do we speak up and when do we jump ship?

These two opposing ideas were helping me to find that middle ground where I wanted to live my life. They were helping me have some understanding of Army mentality and why it's needed.

I'm so independent I can't even imagine such blind obedience, yet I don't want to be totally alone. There are times I want a good leader or teacher. I often get faced with the choice of whether to follow or simply to walk away. There are times to obey and times to forge my own path. There is strength in community and connection, but in my opinion it is enhanced and made stronger as each of us as individuals find our own strength, and as strong individuals we come together with our unique pieces of the puzzle.

CHAPTER 11:

Graduating from Basic Training

A MONTH AFTER THE TOASTMASTERS SPEECH, Gabe was graduating from Basic Training. He was stationed at Fort Sill, Oklahoma. It could get hot there. Two weeks before he got there, two cadets died of heat exhaustion. Before they even started, they were gone. I was glad that the heat wave had passed by the time Gabe arrived.

Gabe had just completed his first two months of Army life. Army training is about being pushed to your limits and learning obedience. Like all the other cadets, he had to dig deep and find strength in himself he never knew he had. He told me it wasn't the big strong men that did best. Some of them caved from the pressure. It was those with deep inner strength and mental fortitude, and at that Gabe excelled.

I was proud of him, even while I was worried and afraid. His graduation was a big moment and I wanted him to know how much he meant to me. I didn't want to miss it. So I bought a plane ticket and flew out to Oklahoma for the ceremony.

My first night, Gabe greeted me in his full dress uniform. I took him to the movies. We saw "The Matrix Revolutions," the third of the Matrix series. We went into the theater in the afternoon, while it was still light outside. By the time we got out we were in an altered reality. In the movie it was dark and pouring rain. I remember a scene where there was water everywhere and it was pouring over an edge and creating a whirlpool. And as we left the theatre the outside world was mirroring what we watched. It was getting dark and rain was pouring down in buckets.

Gabe couldn't get the uniform wet so I ran to get the rental car and pulled it around where he could get in. He needed the uniform for next day's graduation.

I don't know why, but Neo reminds me of Gabe. Maybe it's the era he grew up in and that he loved martial arts. He also loved Sci Fi and Fantasy. I haven't watched the Matrix since that time, but Keanu Reeves will always remind me of Gabe.

The next day was his ceremony. I tried to get intel so I'd know where to be and when, but they wouldn't tell us parents anything. I hated it. It felt like it was how they let everyone know who was in control.

According to Gabe they didn't tell him or anyone else what was going on either. Basic Training is designed to teach blind obedience to orders and part of that training was the practice of never knowing what to expect. In the battlefield they could not anticipate a strike, so the training needed to prepare them for the unknown. At a moment's notice they would be called out for an exercise. It makes sense in training and on the battlefield, but much less sense when used on us parents and family, who were simply trying to get to the event.

I was still trying to wrap my brain around this need of obedience. The speech about the fire drill helped me appreciate the need to follow orders without question. At Gabe's commencement exercise I had a hard time finding him in the hundreds of other soldiers in the group. Like a Borg in Star Trek, they are taught to dress neatly, to not stand out in any way, not even a hair or shoelace out of place. They are one of many.

But I'm fiercely independent. It's hard for me to comply to someone else's blind orders. I had that inner struggle going on throughout the ceremony.

I got to the barracks early. Without more information, it was the best I could do. Gabe showed me their room and his bed. It wasn't long before we left for the ceremony.

I found a seat and soon the graduation began. We were led in the Pledge of Allegiance. The soldiers rose to stand at attention, all hundred or more at once, with a loud "humph". The power of that group movement reverberated through the entire room. They sat back down in the same way. Later we went outside and watched the marches. They carried that same group energy, it was an energy so much more powerful than one-plus-one-plus-one to a hundred. The power of the group was beyond any individual there.

I still couldn't spot Gabe in the crowd. With the intention of everyone looking alike it was hard to find him, but I finally did. I watched as he marched up, walked across the stage and received his certificate. But it wasn't passive for me. Graduations impact me more than weddings. I've been there for every graduation of my daughters and of my grandkids. Every time I am moved by how proud I feel for each of them. The graduation marks a completion of working towards something. It's an achievement. They're ready to go forward with the next step in their life.

Gabe's Basic Training Graduation trumped them all. I watched the films as they showed the cadets practicing military moves. It hit me that my baby, Gabe (and I suddenly really wanted him to still be my baby) was going to be in live action doing those things for real. My boy wasn't my baby any more. I couldn't keep him at home or watch over what he did. I couldn't keep him safe. He was growing up, not just going off to a job and moving out of the house: he was going off to war.

The next day he had a free day, and we spent it together. I took him out to a buffalo preserve. In a few days Gabe would leave for his training with the 82nd Airborne at Fort Bragg, North Carolina. This is where he'd be stationed until they sent him off for active duty. When the day was over I dropped him back at the barracks and drove away. I was on my way back home.

CHAPTER 12:

Coming Home to Family

WITH MEMORIES OF GABE'S GRADUATION, I was coming back home to California again. My plane landed and I gathered my things, excited to see my girls. This visit was supposed to be short. I had a return ticket to go back in a few weeks. But two weeks came and went and I didn't leave. Once I was back with my family I realized how much I missed had missed them. I ended up staying almost two years.

Anni needed my help. A few days after I arrived, she asked if I could stay longer to help take care of her new baby. Jordan was seven months by then. After Gabe's death and having her baby Anni had taken the spring and summer off from school. But she had another year and a half to finish at Sac State (Sacramento State University) and needed someone to help out so she could go back to school. She said I could stay in her spare room. I like to help my kids and I was easily persuaded.

Anni's life had also changed in the months after Gabe's death. Her son Jesse was eight, so having the new baby was like being a new mom all over again. Anni and Chris had moved back to the Bay Area and they'd bought a house in Concord. She was living closer to her old friends, but it meant she had over an hour commute to Sacramento for school.

I was enjoying the company of my kids and grandkids again. I wanted more time together to reconnect and heal. We all had our different ways of working through our grief, but it felt good to be there to support each other. Heidi and her family were back in the area, too. She had a new boyfriend, Dave, and they were living in Lafayette.

When Gabe was in Afghanistan he wasn't happy that I was living in Mexico. I had moved there after he was already in the Army. My first year in Mexico, when Gabe came home for Christmas, I couldn't afford to fly back. He was there, my girls were there, but I didn't have the money. I sent gifts instead. That was right before he was shipped to Afghanistan.

Looking back, I can see now why he didn't like me being there. He felt ungrounded, with no house to come home to. He was worried about me. Most people think Mexico is more dangerous than the US, though I don't find it that way. I actually feel more of a societal anger, stress and conflict when I'm in the US. There seems to be less patience and more road rage. But my safety there was still one of Gabe's concerns.

At the time I couldn't understand his issues. This was the first real adventure of my life and I needed to do it for me, so I pushed his feelings aside and did the best I could. Now that Gabe was dead and I was back home, I felt like I needed to somehow make it up to my family.

The lessons of Tezcatlipoca helped me make some sense of things, but that was only the beginning of getting a grip on how to cope with my Gabe's death. I was still grieving.

I was glad to have my baby granddaughter to take care of. I enjoyed her immensely. I've always loved being around babies, especially my babies and grandbabies. Being a mother and grandmother comes naturally to me, like it's part of my soul purpose.

I watched Jordan grow into a toddler and I loved being with her and seeing it all. She went from scooting to crawling to pulling herself up on the furniture and walking. She started communicating, first with grunts and sounds, then with her first words. Her personality began showing through.

Then Heidi got pregnant again. Dave was the dad. They made a good couple. I met Dave when I first got back and immediately it felt like he was part of our family. Now they were having a baby together. The following September, when their baby was born, I was there with them. They decided to name him Gabriel, after his uncle. (This wasn't the first or last baby that was named after Gabe.)

There were mornings when a pregnant Heidi and I would go for walks, pushing baby Jordan in a stroller. We'd talk about all sorts of things. Often the conversation would drift to Gabe.

One of our favorite places to walk was an old road that used to go from Martinez to Port Costa, a path I had hiked when I lived in the area years before. It worked well with the stroller because it's mostly still paved. But the road is closed and no longer used for cars. Too many parts of it have eroded away. So now it's just for walking.

Heidi told me how she felt about her brother. "He never bought big gifts for the kids. He didn't think they needed more stuff," she said. "But he always made sure to spend time with each of us in a way that was special and meaningful."

"I'm so glad I came home for his last visit," I said. "I wasn't sure if I was going to. He was upset with me for living in Mexico. And the leave before that he spent so much of his time with his friends, I guess I felt neglected. I just wasn't sure if I should come."

"That last visit was special." Heidi said. "He made sure he spent time with each of us. I remember our talks. He told me about things he was worried about. I think he looked up to me a lot, because I was his big sister."

As we walked we shared those special memories. Then we'd get to where the trail was washed out. We either had to carry the stroller and the baby across or turn back. So this is where we turned around.

During those two years I tried to make California my home again. My things in Mexico were packed away and it didn't really matter if or when I went back. I needed to start earning money again, too. I hadn't had a job since I took off for Mexico and when I was there I had a trade arrangement where I lived. I helped out in exchange for room and board. I loved the freedom. I also led some workshops and did healing work on the side. But being in the US was more expensive and life didn't work in trade, at least not where I was. I needed money.

I started finding more work as a freelance web designer. Anni helped me get a few clients. I liked it because it was something I could do from anywhere. I couldn't see myself conforming to a 9 to 5 job any more or setting my life by someone else's schedule.

But I still felt pulled in diametrically opposite directions. The life I'd been living in Mexico was so different and I missed it. I felt like I was living someone else's idea of what my life should be, not one of my own choosing. Yet, family was important, too.

In Mexico we held sweat lodges. I had been to vision quests. In the Bay Area I struggled to find somewhere between the busy lives of those around me and my need for deeper connection, both inside and out.

CHAPTER 13:

My First Sweat Lodge

MY LIFE HAD ITS OWN TRAJECTORY, quite different from Gabe's or my daughters'. While Gabe was joining the Army, getting his training and shipping off to Afghanistan, I was growing and learning new things for myself. Though Gabe wanted to be a warrior, I was interested in peace. As a kid I thought that "Indians" were cool. I never related to cowboys, other than that they had horses. I never liked guns. I would have loved to live in the mountains and camp all the time.

Around the time Gabe enlisted and I still lived in Northern California, I attended my first ever sweat lodge. I'd always been interested in knowing more about Native American people and their ceremonial practices, but I was an outsider who didn't know how to get in.

This changed when I moved to Ashland, Oregon, and then Hornbrook, California. I started connecting with people who held ceremony on a regular basis. I got my in when I volunteered to help with the Ashland Country Fair and Steve, the fair organizer, invited me to a sweat lodge.

Steve picked me up and we drove out to the Marble Mountains in Northern California. We were headed to a remote ranch nestled in the Quartz Valley. I met Charlie Redhawk Tom, the medicine man. He was an 84-year-old man, and yet, still running sweat lodges regularly. Charlie wasn't at all what I expected. He had a big, open heart that made me feel welcome and set me at ease.

The sweat lodge was built by the side of a creek. We stood around chatting while the fire tender laid the logs for a large bonfire. I watched as he placed river stones over the logs. Charlie led a ceremony and prayer as the fire was lit and blazed to life. It was perhaps an hour or two more before the fire burned down and the stones were ready. I think this was my first introduction to what they call "Indian Time," which means everything happens in its right time, in the natural order of things. There was no rush and nothing was pushed. Indian Time (like Mexican time) is a way of being with the world that my Western mind wasn't used to.

Everything about the ceremony was new to me, but Charlie and Steve explained what we were doing. First we were smudged with sage to clear any negative energy from our field. As we entered the rounded dome of the sweat lodge I was instructed to bend down, put my head on the ground, and say *"O Mitakuye Oyasin"*, meaning "to all my relations". This honors our connection to all of life, the plants and animals, the stones, water and earth.

The inside of the lodge was lined with straw. I was told to enter to the right and to crawl around until I came to the person before me and then sit. Per Steve's instructions, I wore a light dress and brought a towel. The towel was to cover my face when the steam got too hot.

Once everyone entered, Charlie came in last. The hot stones from the fire were carried in on a pitchfork and placed in an indented circle in the center. The enclosed space quickly began to heat.

Charlie told us a little of what to expect: "We close the door and we will sing songs and offer our prayers to the Grandfather Fire," he said. "There are four doors. That means we will open the door four times. When it's open you can go out."

"It will get hot and you will sweat. When it gets too hot you can lie down on the straw, it's cooler by the floor. The heat rises, so it helps to get your head down. If it's too hot call out for us to open the door. If it's still too hot and we don't open the door fast enough, make your own door out the side"

To make your own door would be fitting your way between the willow branches that made the frame and then pushing your way through several layers of blankets that covered the lodge.

I later learned that Charlie had made his own door once, but because he was a big, round man, he got stuck halfway between in and out, perhaps a bit like Winnie the Pooh when he got stuck in his hole after eating too much honey.

I loved Charlie's light humor. I had come with an image of ceremony being strict, making sure everything was done just right. I think he taught me that the best medicine is love and humor.

The sweat lodge was hotter than I imagined. When they closed the door Charlie placed medicine herbs on the rocks and then he poured on water. Sweat immediately poured down my face and from all parts of my body. The steam was incredible. I felt it burning my skin. I was glad for the towel to offer some protection. Yet, when Charlie started drumming and singing, I followed along and joined in. I took my turn saying my prayers. And when it was finally over I felt lighter than a feather.

This first native ceremony seemed to awaken a primal connection in me to the ways of the land. I wanted more.

CHAPTER 14:

Vision Quest

THAT SAME SUMMER I GOT INVITED to be a "right hand" for my friend, Snowflower, who was doing a vision quest. The right hand is a helper who supports the person out on their quest. I felt honored. Of course I went.

At the week-long vision quest ceremony I learned much more about indigenous ways. Our group worked together and everyone participated in camp chores. We all helped to set up and take down the camp. Together we did the cooking, washed dishes, built and tended fire. We took turns watching the sacred fire that energetically supported Snowflower and another quester while they were out *"on the hill."* There was also a group campfire and we'd gather around it each night and share our experiences in a talking circle.

On our last day we had *"giveaway."* The questers gifted the people who helped support them on their quest. Some of their gifts were special offerings they picked out for each person who had helped them. It was kind of like Christmas, but the gifts had deeper meaning. Part of a quester's giveaway was to gift each item they had with them on their quest to someone else in the group. Through the quest these items had become sacred and they were passed on to the next year's questers.

I had decided I wanted to quest the next year. This new life called to me, like it was something I'd always been missing to make me more whole. I just hadn't known it. My only rites of passage into adulthood had been moving out on my own at 18 and getting a job, followed quickly with getting married and having kids. When I saw what questing was about I longed for the experience for myself.

Teri was the leader of the group and had been facilitating vision quests for about ten years. She'd had years of apprenticeship and learning before that. She demonstrated love and compassion with everyone there. Teri took the time to explain what the ceremony was about, every step of the way. Her wisdom went deep.

She accepted me as a quester for the following year. In the giveaway my friend, Snowflower, gave me her sleeping bag and tarp. It was my turn next.

My first quest was to be in Arizona. Teri met with me monthly for a full year of preparation. I tied a chain of prayer ties, seven prayers for each day of the year, a chain of 2,555 prayers in total.

Teri was my consultant and teacher. She asked me to start journaling about my dreams and helped me look at them to see what they were about. She applied them to what was going on in my life to help me identify the theme of my quest.

When summer came, I was off to Arizona. I brought my oldest granddaughter, Julia, to help support me. We were supposed to have two supporters, but I couldn't find anyone else to be there for me. She was only ten. It was a whole new world for her and everyone loved her.

Our group came from different parts of the country and as we arrived we all helped set up camp. The next day Teri opened the ceremony with prayers and lighting the sacred fire. Then it was time to take me out to my spot. I had chosen my own sacred place to quest the day before. It was away from camp, but where our security could check on me. I brought everything with me that I'd need for my three to four days out. I had my sleeping bag, a bottle of water to drink, and my tarp. I brought my sacred objects, prepared throughout the year. Teri set the energy for my space, using the prayer ties to form a protective circle around me where I would stay throughout my quest.

There was one other quester that year, other than me. He had his own spot, but I never saw it. I felt supported in a way I'd never known before, knowing that the people in camp were tending the sacred fire and holding space for me and the other quester while we were *"out on the hill."*

As questers we fasted and prayed, asking for our vision or sacred song. I'm not one of those people who often have the big, profound moments of spiritual awakening. I rarely see visions. My awareness is more subtle, a simple knowing or feeling. But my knowing and intuition can be harder to trust and I wonder if I'm just making things up. Sometimes I think it's my expectation and hope that keep the spiritual gifts elusively out of my reach.

So, even after three days of fasting, I wasn't sure if I'd gotten what I was there to get. But I did feel different when I came back to camp. I had a stronger sense of purpose and even more urgency to step into it. I also had a new totem animal join me. There were dragonflies hanging out on the trees and flying around me while I sat in my circle. Dragonfly is considered a symbol of transformation.

Over time, I've learned that the power of ceremony isn't just what shows up while you're in ceremony. It goes much deeper. It changed me from the inside out. I could see a change in how I related to the world and to my friends and family. I had begun my transformation.

CHAPTER 15:

A Modern Day Rite of Passage

I THOUGHT OF MY VISION QUEST and rites of passage as I was trying to come to terms with Gabe's choice to be a soldier. The first few times he came home on leave I tried talking him into deserting and running to Canada, where many conscientious objectors to the Vietnam war went to escape the draft in the 1960s and '70s. . But he wouldn't do it. He made his choice, and even if he didn't like it, he wasn't quitting. At that point I think he still liked some things about it; he hadn't gotten to the point of hating it yet.

I respected his honor and that he wasn't a quitter. Being in the Army had made him a better person. I accepted his choice, but it never got any easier.

I think Gabe needed the Army to prove himself. He needed to test himself, to push his limits. He grew up fast in the Army and became so much more of who he was.

As I'd learned from the vision quest, it's common for boys (more often boys than girls) in native or indigenous cultures to go through a rite of passage when coming of age. They are sent out into the wilderness, away from their families and communities, away from all they know. Often walking for days on end, without food or shelter, they quest for insight and meaning for their life. When they pass their ordeal they return to the village as men, now recognized as adults in their community. Ceremonies and rituals accompany their return, celebrating their change into manhood.

The ordeal of the quest pushes them in ways they had never been pushed. It requires the boy to find inner strength and go past his perceived limits. It becomes a proving ground, where he discovers himself and is changed in the process. And he then knows himself in a new way. I had discovered this for myself and I knew what the process could do.

These kinds of experiences are powerful. They have a way of stripping away the ego and the illusion of self to reveal a deeper connection and knowing of who we are.

But these Rites of Passage have mostly been lost in the modern world. I think our young men (and women) suffer because of it. They search for ways to prove themselves and to know they are worthy. I think it's one reason why gangs are popular with inner city kids. They find a connection and a community where they prove and know themselves, a place they can be seen.

For Gabe, like many other young men, I think he found it in the Army. Gabe left for Basic Training in July 2003. I was there the day the recruiter came to pick him up. He was flown to Portland for some initial paperwork and immunizations. His first ordeal was the smallpox vaccine. He wrote home and told me that it made him so sick he suffered all through the first week of basic training.

His basic training was in Fort Sill, Oklahoma. With all the other cadets, he was pushed physically, mentally and emotionally. In every way, basic training turns these young boys into men and like any ordeal of endurance, he hated it. Yet, eight weeks after he left home, I flew to Oklahoma to be there for his graduation and I could see the difference. He had grown into a confident young man who knew himself better and had proved his strength.

Of course, my own resistance kicked in as well. It was hard to see him grow in this way. They were teaching my son, my baby, to use a gun, lethally if needed. He was taught to obey and respond immediately to drills. Even after the graduation ceremony, on the one free day we had together, he had to sleep at the barracks and wake up at 4:00 am for a forced march.

I cried all throughout his graduation ceremony. Graduations always make me cry, but this one wasn't just the pride I felt, it was tinged with the grief that my son had to become a war machine and it scared me. I knew the danger he would be in when called to go to war.

Even though I hated to admit it, it seemed the Army gave Gabe the environment he needed to prove himself as a warrior. I didn't want him in the Army, but it was what he chose for himself. It was his way.

CHAPTER 16:

Learning Ceremony

WHILE I WAS BACK IN CALIFORNIA, I was also learning a different kind of ceremony. Ceremony had become an integral part of my life in Mexico. It was all around me. Aztec dancers would come to the plaza in our small town of Amatlán and perform, dressed up in full feathered headdresses and colorful regalia. At the retreat center where I lived we held a sweat lodge ceremony almost every weekend. The ancient ways of purification were important in Mexican culture.

Before I'd left Northern California for my big adventure that got me living in Mexico I had taken a few classes with Teri, the lady who had guided me on my vision quest. The first was called *"The Art of Ceremony"* and there was another about *"Shamanic Journeying."* We practiced deep, meditative journeys and connected to our animal totems, past lives, lost parts of ourselves and spirit guides. I learned to see myself as a multidimensional being with helpers all around me. The classes were all part of a Ministerial Apprenticeship I was working towards.

By the fall of 2008, when I was still living at the retreat center in Amatlán, I got invited by Teri to participate in an apprenticeship program for a women's ceremony. This ancient ceremony was connected to water, the full moon and our feminine womb. It felt right. In Mexico I had been given the spiritual name Ixchel, after the Goddess Ix'Chel, the Mayan goddess of water and the moon. Ix'Chel is known as the Mother Goddess, connected to all of creation and especially childbirth and fertility. This ceremony and my new name felt like they fit together and were part of my spiritual calling.

I also wanted to get better at being a leader and sharing these practices I loved in a group with others. Rather than being the bystander, I wanted to be one of those people offering the ceremony. I was hoping the apprenticeship would help me with that.

The classes started in November. As with Teri's other classes, we met over the phone and got recordings and handouts. We explored the definition of ceremony and what it could mean in our lives. This class taught me what women's power was and helped me understand the concept of Sacred or Divine Feminine.

I soaked up everything Teri taught us. Her classes gave me access to learning something I hadn't found available anywhere else. I am not Native American or Mexican. I didn't grow up with these indigenous teachings and had no access to them. Teri was part Cherokee and had learned through her own apprenticeship. She blended both worlds.

I had no idea what Sacred Feminine meant. I only had a vague idea what it meant to access my power as a woman. I had been viewing the world from a masculine perspective. That became even more clear when we started our apprenticeship.

When I first heard of it I wasn't even drawn to a ceremony that was just for women. I like to be very inclusive. The way I saw it, anyone that feels they want to be part of something should have the opportunity to join in. That probably developed from my upbringing and my life where I could never find my way to fit. I don't want others to feel that way. I don't want anyone to feel pushed aside.

I didn't really get why women needed their own path. I had attended a women's group once when I lived in Ashland, Oregon. It felt like just a bunch of women complaining about how men treated us. I didn't feel empowered. It certainly didn't get me in touch with being a woman.

I found Teri's classes were different. She talked about the aspects of the sacred feminine: compassion, intuition, connection, the darkness and the night, the womb. The feminine is nurturing. She holds space for her family and loved ones, a space for them to grow to their potential.

Teri told us about the tribe in which these ceremonies were once held. These practices for connecting to the womb had developed over hundreds of years. The women held this ceremony with every full moon. They would come to the women's lodge, down by the river, and gather water in a large granite bowl. The bowl represented the womb and our connection, as women, to the water. The women would share their stories, their challenges, their problems, even problems they had with each other. The places where they would rub up against each other and have friction were all brought to the circle.

Unlike some spiritual practices, this path doesn't ignore feelings. Instead of gossiping, feelings were felt, expressed and shared. The energies were held together in the unlimited potential of the womb. And in compassion and love they shifted and changed to their highest expression. We all want to be our divine selves, and in holding space for that suchness, we find our way there.

The feminine is a subtle energy, though she can also be as fierce as a mother bear. I realized that I had been trying to be seen by others in a way that was much more masculine. It was the way of the world. There is so much effort to be the loudest and be seen as bigger, better, more important than anyone else. It's a very competitive way of being. And all my life I tried to play that game. It was exhausting.

Yet, my true nature wanted cooperation, not competition. I didn't want to try talking louder or make the best argument just to be seen. I wanted peace, not war. Understanding, not alienation.

When I learned to use these practices I became much more aware that my feminine power, even if it wasn't seen, was felt by others and they were drawn to it. I learned that as I connected more to who I wanted to be, to the true self inside me, more people noticed me, paid attention to what I said and saw me for who I was. I fell in love with myself and loved being a woman.

These classes continued every month for nine months. At the time I didn't see why it had to take so long. I wanted to be told the steps of leading ceremony and then just do it. And we did start holding and practicing our own ceremonies during that year. But we still had to commit to and attend the full nine months. By the end of that time, by the time we were initiated the following October, I realized I had changed so deeply within, it was about much more than just learning the steps of the ceremony. True apprenticeship takes time and transformation.

CHAPTER 17:

Handling Grief, My Way

THE WOMEN'S RETREAT AND INITIATION was held near Reno, just a few hours from where I was living with Anni and her family. When I got back from the retreat Anni was getting close to completing school and I was trying to decide my next move.

I still struggled to navigate my grief. I really had no roadmap or plan. This was all new for me. In the years of living in Ashland, Oregon, Mount Shasta, California and then Tepoztlán in Mexico, I had made great strides in finding myself. But now I was lost, in a land of lost souls. No one else seemed to grasp what grieving was about.

The practice of holding space that I'd learned in my women's ceremonies was helping. I knew I couldn't just ignore my feelings, I needed to feel them. I practiced the holding meditations we'd learned. They gave me a way to hold myself through the pain.

None of it was easy. I loved my son and it hurt so much to have him gone. It made no sense that my life could keep moving forward without him.

I wasn't done grieving just because the funeral was over. Our society seems to think we should just move on, especially after that first year. But missing my son is something that will be with me the rest of my life.

I didn't know how to talk about it with others. I felt awkward bringing it up. In normal conversation I'd often be asked ask me how many kids I had and I didn't know how to answer. Sometimes I'd say: "I have two daughters." Other times I'd get bold with: "I had three kids, but my son died in Afghanistan." They would answer with: "I'm so sorry." And then we'd move on. I didn't know what else to say.

My friends would tell me that Gabe was in a better place and I shouldn't feel sad. I'd think, *"What? Really? I loved my son and I'm sad that he's gone."*

I know they meant well, but it just wasn't helpful. Feeling my feelings was important to me. Gabe might even be in a better place, I hope he is. But I'm still here without him and my feelings matter. I don't believe in stuffing them down to make others more comfortable.

I couldn't find any solace in talking to people who really had no idea what I was going through, but felt they knew what was best for me. So rather than subject myself to unwanted advice, I quit talking about it. I withdrew further into myself.

The New Age community seemed to be the hardest for me to be around. One day I met a friend at a local coffee shop for tea. He was a new acquaintance and I was looking forward to getting to know him better.

We chatted for a while. He told me he lives out of his RV, traveling around the country. I liked that. The gypsy life was appealing to me. I wanted to get ideas about living a simple lifestyle for myself.

But I guess he picked up on something in my mood. He said, "You see a bit down. Why is your energy so low?"

"My son died last year," I said.

He was an avid student of the Law of Attraction. "You just need to raise your vibration." he said. "You will feel better when your vibration is higher."

I didn't know how to respond. I thought, "If you're feeling down, how do you start thinking and feeling thoughts that are higher to raise that vibration? Am I really supposed to ignore my feelings?"

It was obvious this guy didn't have much money, but if he was so good at following his own Law of Attraction advice he should be flowing with abundance. That's kind of what it's about. But, even though he wasn't living a perfect life, he was telling me what I was doing wrong.

I tried changing the subject. I know enough about the Law of Attraction to understand how it works. I also know it's important to feel how I feel. Not acknowledging my feelings is just a bypass. And no one can know what's right for me, or know how I feel, better than myself. Especially someone who has never had a son or experienced deep grief.

But I wasn't interested in arguing my cause. I didn't have the energy or strength to fight off his unwanted advice. It's too bad that at our weakest times we often get the most unfeeling advice. Instead, I quit talking to him about it and left as quickly as I could.

He was just one example of the kind of people I'd run across. Not everyone was like that. But there were enough of them that I learned to withdraw and isolate myself even more.

Of course there were other options for dealing with my feelings, like grief counseling or church. But they didn't feel right, either. I live a spiritual life, but I am not religious and I couldn't start going to church when it wasn't a fit. And I've never found counseling that worked for me. I didn't need to tell someone I didn't know about how I felt and I didn't need that same someone telling me how to grieve. I don't fit the norms and giving me textbook advice that doesn't fit the unique way I see the world doesn't appeal to me.

Another friend suggested that I talk to a friend of hers who had lost her son in war. But that was when it was all so fresh. I wasn't ready to make friends with someone I didn't know based solely on the common grounds of our sons' deaths. In the beginning I don't think I was ready to share my son, especially with people I didn't know.

I have been a loner most my life and I was used to handling life on my own. So reaching out wasn't something I really thought of. Rather than helping me connect, these kind of responses kept me from talking to others and I became more isolated than ever.

CHAPTER 18:

Grieving Ritual

I HAD NEVER THOUGHT OF GRIEVING AS A RITUAL. It wasn't what I grew up with and my family wasn't into that sort of thing. But then a friend loaned me the book, *"Of Water and the Spirit: Ritual, Magic, and Initiation in the Life of an African Shaman,"* by Malidoma Patrice Some. Malidoma wrote of the various rituals performed in his Dagara village in Africa. They had rituals for everything. One was for grieving.

One thing that appealed to me throughout the story was the view of his village life. The village worked through everything that happened in their lives through community rituals. When someone cheated or stole from someone, they didn't just cheat on their partner or take from another, it affected the community. They also celebrated life together.

The rites of passage were done with all the young men and their stepping into adulthood was honored by all. The grieving ritual was the same way. People weren't left to feel their grief alone. The loss was communal and processed in a community ritual.

I'd been so alone with my grief, I missed that connection of community, even though that kind of village life was something I'd never had. How could we bring African rituals or community life into the world we live in? Perhaps, like the ceremonies I had learned, there were ways to blend aspects into our modern life. But I didn't know how.

I became very interested in the idea of a grieving ritual. But I didn't know if Malidoma's style of grieving was right for me, either. He wrote of the ritual being held over a prolonged period, with days of wailing. I grew up in a much more repressed society and although I've come a long way in learning to open and express my feelings, openly wailing feels forced and uncomfortable to me.

I looked up Malidoma's website. He was offering apprenticeship in ritual and ceremony. I was interested, but it was a big commitment of time. And the cost was high. Then, I found that he was offering a grieving ritual. I still wasn't sure his style would work for me, but I thought maybe I'd try. The problem was, it was only being held on the East Coast that year, adding a flight and lodging into the mix. I couldn't afford it. So, I forgot about it and got on with my life. There were plenty of things that needed my attention, just in the daily course of living, and figuring out how to grieve took a back seat.

Yet the seed was planted. I would have loved a grieving ritual where I could openly share and express my grief with a community. I definitely would have loved being with others that could understand and hold space for me. I could share my support with others that were experiencing and expressing grief of their own. What I didn't want more of were the empty and unfeeling statements of others telling me what to think or feel or how to act.

CHAPTER 19:

Questing Again in Colorado

THREE YEARS HAD GONE BY and I was now splitting my time equally between Mexico and California. As summer came, I was coming back to the states again. First I'd fly to Colorado for my vision quest (I had decided to quest again), then on to Utah for a family reunion, all before returning to California.

I packed my bags for the three flights. My prayer ties went in. I'd been working on them all year, just like I'd done for my first vision quest, but this time I hadn't put enough time aside for my prayers and I came up short. I packed my camp skirts. Quest is a ceremony and the women wore dresses each day. Since I was questing I also needed my sleeping bag, a tarp, and the clothes I would quest in. Everything from my circle would be given away at the end.

This was my second vision quest with Teri, six years after my first. I was part of the community by then. I'd attended all but one year of SpiritQuest since that first time when I was just a right hand. I volunteered on the board of directors for our group and helped with planning our annual quests. Teri was also my teacher for our Women's Ceremonies. I worked with her and our leadership team to put a website together. These people were like my spiritual family, and I'd come to know them deeply.

I had evolved over the years. This time I had friends to support me. First was Kim. She apprenticed with me in the Women's Ceremonies and over the years of coming to Quest she had become a good friend. She was flying in from Sedona. My other supporter was a massage therapist from the Bay Area. Laura and I had met the year after Gabe died. We were both expecting grandsons at the same time. When I was in the area I went to her for massage and healing and I built her a website in trade. This kind of experience was a bit new for her, but she agreed to come support me.

I flew into Colorado from the jungles of Mexico. That morning I waded a stream, with my suitcase in tow, to catch a taxi into town. I'd been on a different type of quest the day before, spending a night under a cliff overhang, in a rainstorm, just above a pyramid for the grandmother of Quetzalcoatl. We took peyote and our guide, Leo, helped us each find a spot and build a fire of our own. Most people stay awake all night with the peyote medicine. It put me to sleep. I was aware when it started raining. I felt the mountain shake with thunder and saw the water dripping just past my overhang. Throughout the night I would stir as Leo came to check on me and build up my fire. I would pull my poncho around me for warmth. I slept under the overhang, feeling held by the mother energy of the earth.

I still felt the effects as the plane landed at the Denver Airport. Teri and her husband picked me up. They rolled my big suitcase onto the white carpets in their house, leaving a streak of dried mud. I felt dirty, like a jungle rat, in their pristine home. Yet, my friends embraced me like family. We knew each other and I was welcomed into their fold. Being greeted by my friends felt like coming home to a different kind of family, my soul family.

The next few days I gathered with Teri, her husband, and our other board members, meeting for business and enjoying some time together as friends. A couple days later the other people flew in and we headed for the mountains.

I'd learned a few things over the years. When Teri set the sacred circle for the fire she told us the East Door was the only opening. Because it was the weakest part of the circle, it was traditionally guarded by a "blooded warrior", a warrior who had drawn blood in protection of his people, perhaps even killed another. We had security at camp. We'd usually have a man for this position, sometimes a woman warrior. This person would energetically hold the East Door, even when they weren't present in person. But when she told us about the tradition of the "blooded warrior" I that I knew that Gabe was also there. He was a true "blooded warrior" and he held the energy for us.

From that moment, I knew that Gabe was always there at Quest with us. I felt safer knowing that he was watching over me. I began to think of him more and more as my spirit warrior, I would call on him at times when I felt I needed a little extra protection.

For the past several years I'd helped out at Quest and the year before this I was asked to be Camp Mom. It felt like a natural fit, much like what I did at the retreat center in Mexico. But when I got there the weight of responsibility overwhelmed me. For the first time in my life I didn't have the energy to hold that space for others. I needed to stretch out and ask for help and our community came through. I divvied up the chores and our week went smoothly.

That year we'd been near Reno, Nevada and Cindy was doing her Elder quest. She was a blind lady who had incredible insight. At giveaway she gave me her bag. I was my turn to quest again.

This year in Colorado was different for me. I would be surrounded and supported by my friends, but I hardly had time to visit with them. I was questing. My focus was on my journey. I'd be away on the hill for most the time.

We drove from Denver, about 45 minutes past Boulder and up into high alpine forests. Our quest was at a scout camp called Calwood. With elevations of 8,000 ft., it was higher than we'd been previous years. It got cold at night.

I found my spot on the slope of a hill, a little further out than my first quest, but still within walking distance of camp. The tarp I used was Gabe's army poncho. He would watch over me and guard my circle. Those days and nights on the mountain were quiet and peaceful, a getaway from the pressures of life. A hummingbird kept flying around my spot. I'd been given the name of Chuparosa (meaning Hummingbird in Spanish) by an elder in Mexico. It signified sucking the nectar or joy of life. I felt ready for more joy.

I stayed out on the hill for three nights. Although I felt good, and perhaps even a bit altered, I wasn't getting any aha's or enlightened experience. I wondered if this kind of questing is just not my way. On my first quest I thought maybe I just wasn't doing it right or going deep enough. But this time I had more experience. I've learned that meditation for some people is quietly going within, for others the transformative experience is found in movement such as walking. Walking has always appealed to me. Maybe that's the lesson the hummingbird wanted me to see. The hummingbird never stops moving; if it is caged it will slowly die.

I decided after three days and uncomfortable nights on the hill, I had received what I needed and walked back into camp. I did as previously instructed, walking directly to the sacred fire and keeping my face down, not making eye contact with my friends. Kim and Laura were at the fire. One went to get Teri for my debriefing.

Teri asked me about my quest. Did I have any insights? Was there anything connected to the dreams I'd had? Or my journaling in my preparations for quest?

My thoughts were not very coherent. I hadn't eaten for three days. "I still feel it's important to do my work. It's time to get it out in the world." I said. "My work is guiding others to find their true calling or true self."

Teri replied with, "I need to tell you what happened back here at camp. A wind gusted through while your two supporters, Kim and Laura, were tending the sacred fire. It blew the awning out of its stakes, picked it up and moved it about ten feet. They had to grab at it. Just before the wind came the two of them had been talking about something and it seems they were arguing or upset." (This is a no-no at sacred fire. We are asked to keep our thoughts and talking focused on positive things, since the energy can carry to the questers.)

This was a lot to take in. Laura had a big family back at home and a lot of responsibilities as a mother and grandmother. Perhaps it had something to do with that.

But Teri responded, "These were your two supporters. This must have represented something you were going through or something you need to know. Do you have any idea what it would be?"

"I had a pretty quiet time on the mountain," I told her. "It was peaceful and relaxed."

She suggested I meditate with it. From the shamanic perspective everything means something and she insisted that the meaning had to do with me. But I didn't feel any truth in that. Isn't it possible that sometimes a rock is just a rock? Or even if this had meaning, was her interpretation always correct? I felt like it had more to do with what Kim and Laura were talking about or working through. It didn't really feel fair that I was supposed to take responsibility for this.

It reminded me of the times people told me that I had anger I had to get out and process when I didn't feel any anger at all. (These weren't times I was showing upset, when anger might be obvious, but advice people were giving that this was something they thought I needed to work on.) Sometimes I feel people are projecting their ideas on me. I've had psychic readings and other advice where it was quite obvious the issue was the other person's, not mine. I think it's why I tend to be a loner; it's not that I always like being alone, I just don't like people telling me what they think is right for me. I need to discover that for myself. It seems like that is the purpose of a vision quest: to find my own inner truth.

Despite my frustration with Teri's ideas, I was happy to be back in camp. The community formally welcomed me and the other quester back in. I was still integrating, whereas the rest of the group had spent the week together. It felt odd to not be more involved with the others. I had missed the nights by the fire, the community meals and chores, and the nightly talking circles. I felt like I didn't really know what was going on. But still it was sweet to be back.

I got to break my fast, though at first I didn't feel very hungry. That evening I again joined the talking circle. These were my favorite times. We each had our turn to share and explore our feelings, speaking deep from our heart.

Like our other quests, our last night was giveaway. I gave gifts to those who supported me: Teri, Kim, Laura and the others. Gabe's poncho went to the security man who had watched over me. He was an ex-cop from Ashland. He knew what giving blood for others meant.

The week was over. We all helped with tearing down camp, then climbed into our cars. On our way back into Boulder my cell phone kicked back on. I saw several messages from my daughter, Heidi. I listened to them but they didn't make much sense. They had something to do with Julia, her oldest daughter, and something about Julia's dad's other kids.

When we got closer into Boulder and I could get reception I called Heidi back. I couldn't grasp it all at first, as my mind started coming back to the real world. Then it unraveled. Jason, Julia's dad, had two other kids, Riley and Brennan (8 and 6). They had been playing in the backyard pool, the above ground kind that has about four feet of water. The cover was pulled to the side, but the kids were playing in it and one of them got stuck. They speculated that the older one tried to help the younger one, but they both drowned.

I was still in the car with three of my friends from quest. We were going into Boulder for dinner with the group and then on to the airport. When we arrived at the restaurant I told everyone what happened. I could barely eat. I hurt for my granddaughter, losing her brother and sister. I felt for her dad, and even more for her stepmom, a woman I never met. She had been in the house, getting ready to join them in the pool, when it happened. It brought back all my pain of losing my son.

I was glad to be with supportive friends. They listened to me. We prayed together for the kids. On my own I said a silent prayer to Gabe. I asked him to watch over the kids and help them adjust to heaven.

CHAPTER 20:

Summer Family Reunion 2011

THAT NIGHT I FLEW OUT OF COLORADO and directly to
Salt Lake, to join my family for a reunion near the
Utah/Idaho border. It had been three years since Gabe died,
but I hadn't seen any of them since his funeral.

I come from a big family with eight kids, all of us
scattered around the country. So it's nice when we can get
together. My sisters Lark, Terri and Jodi were there and my
two brothers, Jason and Derek. The others couldn't make it.
But we also had some of our kids with their kids, four
generations in all.

Family reunions always come with an interesting mix of
emotions. I grew up in a Utah family. We weren't practicing
Mormons, but it was part of our culture and history.
Brigham Young is my great-great-grandfather on my mom's

side and our Spencer Family Reunions went all the way back to include my grandpa's parents. So they got big.

I loved spending time with my Grandma and Grandpa Spencer. All my aunts and uncles and cousins living in Utah would be there. We knew each other well from family parties held all year long and we could play and goof off for hours. But it was Grandpa's brothers and sisters, too. So we had extended family of great aunts and uncles and their kids. So many people, we couldn't possibly know them all.

The reunions were held in the Utah mountains. They were always camping trips. Grandma and Grandpa had a camper. There were a few others with campers or trailers. My aunt and uncle had a pop-up trailer. Each family prepared their own meals, with a shared meal or two at the end. I remember walking past my cousins' camps with jealousy as I smelled the bacon cooking in the morning. We'd be having something like pancakes.

I'd run off with one of my sisters or cousins and find trails that we could explore half the day. If there was a stream or lake nearby we'd splash in the water and cool off. My Grandpa and his brother, my uncles and some of my cousins would ride motorbikes all day long. They'd leave for a trail ride in the morning and return at the end of the day. And there'd be constant dirt bikes and minibikes running through camp as well.

The women would sit around tables doing craft projects. Sometimes we'd have archery for a bit. The guys, my dad included, would play horseshoes. And there was always a treasure hunt for the kids.

When my dad passed away in his sixties my sisters and brothers were spread all over the country so we decided it was time to start a Tucker Family Reunion of the siblings and grandkids of just our mom and dad. Our first was held the year he passed. It was in Utah, where half the family still lived, but we stayed in the Salt Lake Valley at various houses. Our gatherings were based around playing cards or visiting a local attraction. They weren't the same kind of fun.

This time, in 2011, was probably our fourth Tucker reunion. For years I'd been rallying around the idea of a camping reunion like we had growing up. My sister Lark held one at a scout camp in Indiana. It was a pretty cool place, but most of the family just stayed inside, playing cards. The next was my turn. I planned it at a campground at Lake Tahoe, but most of the family said California was too far away. They wanted something less rustic. If they did come, they didn't want to bring a bunch of camping equipment. And mom was getting old. She didn't want to sleep on the ground.

For the 2011 reunion we finally settled on a large cabin that could sleep 20-30 people, and the kids could spread out on the floor. It was big enough it even had a name, Sutters Cabin. In the photos I could see hills behind it and perhaps some promise of hiking trails. Bear Lake was a half hour away. But there were no trees and it looked a bit desolate. Overall, I was less than excited.

I rode with Lark as we drove three hours north, from Salt Lake City, to the cabin near the Utah/Idaho border. We arrived and settled in, each finding our rooms. I shared a bed with Mom.

It's hard for me to want to take a week vacation to sit in a house. I long for mountains and wild and hills and trails. This had none of that. It was a house on an open hill, nothing nearby. I felt like a spoiled kid, throwing an inner tantrum that I wasn't getting my way.

I wanted to enjoy being with my family. We'd grown apart. Lark was the only one that stayed in touch. She and I talked at least weekly. But the others weren't part of my world. I hoped to find some common ground. I think we all did.

I sat in a circle that first day with my sisters and brothers. My brother Jason said he wanted us to find more reasons to be together. He started us out. "We get together for Mom. But what's going to happen when she dies? Will we stop seeing each other? We're family. I want us to be more than that."

We all agreed. We talked about finding our common ground and giving the reunions more priority in our lives. I don't think much was resolved, but at least we cared about being together.

I tried switching my brain around, kind of inverting my expectations of what family reunion was. I lived in nature most of the year. I had jungle all around me. Perhaps my vacation to the family reunion would be the opposite. Maybe

I could compromise for that week to try to come into their world.

We all had our inner turmoils. Derek and his wife, Cindy, were having trouble getting pregnant. After ten years of marriage, they were fostering two sweet, young kids, a brother and sister. They'd grown close and were hoping to adopt them. Derek told me of the boy's traumatic past. He was making real progress in getting him into kindergarten and working with him on his homework. Cindy was closer to the baby. They got her when she was only nine months old. Both children were blossoming under their care.

Jodi had a new husband. They were there with her youngest daughter and stepson. But Jodi's middle son, Brandon, had developed a liver problem due to a hereditary disease that causes blood clotting. His liver swelled up to double its size and wasn't working any more. He had just gone through a transplant and couldn't come to the reunion. He'd be on medication the rest of his life, but he still wasn't out of the woods.

Lark and her son Daemyn were there. Daemyn is transgender. When Lark and I went with my brothers to pick Daemyn up from the airport all they could talk about is not knowing what to call him or what pronouns to use. Midweek I went for a walk with Lark and Daemyn. He told us how hard it was for him to be there. The last time he came to a reunion was before he realized he was a man in a girl's body. They were all playing Dungeons and Dragons at Derek's house. Daemyn wanted to play a male role. He always did at home. But Derek and Cindy wouldn't allow it.

Not in their house. They said that they had a friend who played an opposite gender role and then he ended up being gay. They couldn't let that kind of thing happen.

Mom just wanted all her kids together and getting along, as many of her kids and grandkids as she could get. She wanted to see us all happy.

I showed up with quest and death on my mind. Quest had been a wonderful experience of connecting to my deeper self and God. I'd been through the three-day ordeal of fasting and praying and I felt good about my accomplishment. I would have loved to share that part of my world. Unfortunately, it was one that my family wasn't interested in.

But death is more universal. I needed to talk about my feelings, of how I felt about these deaths in my granddaughter's family. I hadn't seen my mom, or my brothers and sisters in the three years since Gabe's death. As a family, we'd been lucky. We had lost grandparents, and even dad from a stroke at sixty-five, but never anyone young. In our big family of eight kids, twenty grandkids and over thirteen great-grandkids descended from my mom and dad, Gabe was the only one to die.

I wanted to talk about Gabe. I tried bringing it up with my mom, but she changed the subject, she said "Have you heard about Brandon? We should all feel sorry for Jodi and Brandon, for what they are going through."

I didn't know what to say. I love my Mom. I wanted to talk to her about my feelings, not someone else's. I wanted to talk about the hard facts of death, about my son that wasn't ever going to be there again, not my sister's son who still had life, difficult as it was.

Instead we avoided the uncomfortable conversations. In a family where I learned to be quiet, I retreated again. Lark was the sister who communicated with me after Gabe died, the only one that wrote emails and called. I'd go for a walk with her later and then I'd vent the frustration of not being able to talk to my Mom and share what I truly felt.

PART 3

CHAPTER 21:

Moving to the Mountains

AFTER THOSE COUPLE OF YEARS of living at Anni's, I decided I really wanted a home in both Mexico and California, to come and go more often and see my family every summer and on holidays. I needed to get creative to find a way to do it and still live a simple and semi-nomadic life.

Ideally I could find a way to be closer to my kids when I was in the US. But I didn't want to rent an apartment and the city wasn't my thing. I needed more nature. So I tried living in Hornbrook again. I got an old motorhome and bought into a share at a ranch, up near the Oregon border. It gave me a home base when I was in California, but without California prices.

The downside was that my motorhome was small and it was five hours from the family. So, it wasn't really like I was in the area. Hornbrook sits in an open valley about halfway between Ashland, Oregon and Mount Shasta, California, but it isn't even that pretty. It was more like a compromise that didn't meet any of my dreams. I wanted something nicer and closer to my kids.

After a few more years of back and forth I started looking and found a place in Nevada City, two hours away from the Bay Area and my family. Nevada City is a small town in the foothills of the Sierras. It sits close to 2,500 ft., just below snowlines, but where the environment changes from rolling hills covered with oaks to pine forests. My motorhome, which I later upgraded to a 31 ft. trailer with a slide out, sat in a private yard under 50' cedar and pine trees with an open grassy area out front. It was like heaven. I was in Gold Country, but my treasure was waking up to mornings in the Sierras.

The anniversaries of Gabe's death came around again and again. I felt like I was losing touch with my son. But I didn''t want his life to be forgotten. That would be worse than the pain of remembering.

I'd been wanting to write about Gabe since he died, but eight years later I still hadn't started. I felt numb and stuck, like my life wasn't moving forward. I didn't always attribute it to grief, but it was there, under the surface. Perhaps some part of my soul split off and tried to follow Gabe when he did. I felt incomplete. It was time to start my book and delve into my memories.

I've felt so many feelings arise and move through me over the years; it would be easy to think that the healing is done. Yet, grieving has no steady course.

I'd also become isolated and friends had drifted away. I quit talking about the subject. I felt closed off. I went inward for comfort. It was time to reach out more and share my story.

I was inspired by some of the books I read, like *"Wild: From Lost to Found on the Pacific Crest Trail,"* by Cheryl Strayed and *"The Memory of Running,"* a novel by Ron McLarty. I loved the movie *"The Way,"* with Martin Sheen, written by Emilio Estevez. These all told stories of people who processed their grief through a journey. I'm a walker, hiking is my thing. The idea of a longer, drawn out pilgrimage called to me.

The problem was, I just couldn't afford to not work and go on a journey. I'd have to find another way to write my story.

CHAPTER 22:

Life Flowing Backwards

WHEN I MOVED TO NEVADA CITY I had rent to pay so I needed a steady income again. My web design work wasn't reliable and I always needed new clients. So I decided to try telephone audits. It was work I could count on, there was always plenty to do, and it was so much easier to work when I didn't have to drum up the business myself.

It took me back into the world of insurance premium audits, the work I had done for over 20 years when my kids were growing up.

Back then I worked as a field auditor. I covered a territory and drove hours every day, often in busy traffic, to get my audits done. This time I had the advantage of doing them by phone and email, people would send in copies of their records and I'd just summarize the information. That would be easier, I could do the job from basically anywhere, even my house in Mexico.

But there was more to it than that. It was my job to call and bug people until they'd send me their records. People could be tough to deal with. I had to explain what the audit was for, what records we needed and why, and remind them over and over to get their info together and send it in. There were employees to classify and I had to be the enforcer of rules for the insurance company, rules like which employees were clerical vs. shop, which payroll could be excluded and more. And audits would often generate an increased bill for more premium, sometimes with big surprises. I wasn't the good guy.

I never thought I'd go back to this work. Even though I knew the work inside and out, I had given so much of my life to it. In those days of raising my family, work had come first. It cost me fun, quality time with my kids, time I could never get back. When I left it, I thought I was done with it forever.

Still it offered decent pay for my time, with regular and consistent work. I reasoned it out. It didn't have to consume my life; I could do it part time and still have my freedom. Because it was over the phone, I could do it wherever I wanted, whether I was in California or Mexico. And the work wasn't that hard. I already knew how to do it.

The problem was, as I earned more money, my expenses quickly increased to match my income. The water heater in my old RV caught fire and I decided it was time to upgrade.

I bought a newer and nicer trailer. Soon I felt like a hamster on a wheel. More work meant more money. I was caught in a trap. Again.

I let my website clients slide to the backburner as I spent more time on the audit work. Audits had to be done in a certain time and I'd always have a pile that would get behind, so they seemed to need constant attention.

Friends would invite me to go for walks, but I'd decline so I could get more work done. My life started to shrink in around me. Living in a small trailer got even smaller by my not getting out. I was living in the beauty of the mountains, but not enjoying them.

CHAPTER 23:

Gabe's Last Visit Home

I NEVER BROUGHT GABE TO NEVADA CITY. I'd been there before, but I didn't truly discover the area until I moved there in 2011. So it was interesting how many things I'd come across that would remind me of my son. One time I was picking up a friend from the Sacramento Airport. Walking through the airport, I passed by men in army uniforms. I turned my head, knowing they weren't Gabe, but still wishing they were. It reminded me of Gabe's last visit home.

It was in September 2007. He flew into Sacramento where Anni was living at the time. I arrived a day or two earlier and went to pick him up. He came off the plane wearing his dress uniform. Gabe had olive skin with Mexican features he got from the dad he never really knew.

His normally wavy hair was shaved close, a style he preferred even before he joined the Army. He was so handsome.

I gave him a big hug.

"We always fly in our uniform." he said. "It gets us better service and military discounts."

On base in Afghanistan he'd been working out almost daily. At baggage claim he picked up his two heavy duffle bags, strapping one to his chest and the other to his back, and carried them to the car. It was nothing for him.

He showed off his muscle, telling me he was twice the size of when he enlisted, pulling out his old photos to compare. Gabe was never tall. His dad and I were both short, he was lucky to make it to 5 ft. 10 in. Growing up as the small kid in school he liked to be strong, both inside and out.

Heidi was living in Mount Shasta. Gabe rented a car and he drove us the three hours north to go visit her and her kids. She loves the mountains like I do, and she hadn't moved away when Anni and I left the area.

Heidi had three kids. Her youngest was Aliyah, who was only three. When I went to Mexico I missed her the most, probably because she was the baby. She had wild curls and was at the age where everything she said would give me a glimpse into the naive perceptions of a child. I'd tell her I wanted to take her to Mexico with me, but she wasn't having it. No way was she leaving her mom.

She looked up to her uncle. I think he was a hero to all the kids, but on that visit he gave her special attention. We all went out to the river one day for a picnic. Everyone was having fun playing in the water and hopping across the rocks. When the rocks were too far apart Gabe helped Aliyah. He held her hand or carried her across the scary parts.

When we got back to their home Gabe and I sat on the couch. Aliyah came and plopped herself down between us. She turned to Gabe with stars in her eyes and said: "You're so cool!"

Then she turned towards me. She looked a bit stumped. Then she said: "You're so Mexicoey."

We spent a night at Heidi's, then headed back down to Sacramento. Anni was in the middle of moving and she was a few months pregnant. This would be her second baby, but her son was already eight and she'd lost a baby in between, so I didn't want her to strain herself. I helped her pack boxes and get her place cleaned up. I tried to get Gabe to help, but it just wasn't what he wanted to do on his vacation.

Still we had fun together. I took him to see a movie, *Rush Hour 2*. It wasn't what I would have picked, but Gabe loved martial arts and liked watching Jackie Chan.

Most days I'd drop Anni off at school and then she'd let us use her car. But one day I was ready to drop her off and she decided to skip school and hang out with us. We weren't doing anything special, it was more about spending time together. Went to another movie, *Stardust*. I'll always remember those movies as special. After the movie we went to Ikea for some shopping and I found a one dollar hand broom and dustpan combo that I wanted. Gabe bought it for me. Now I think of him whenever I use it.

He took a day or two to drive down to Concord and visit his old buddies and spend time with his daughter. Angela was never far from his mind and he made sure to see her every time he came home.

Gabe needed a new computer so we went to Fry's. He hated the old computer he had, which kept turning off and not charging. He said he wanted to throw it off a bridge. He ended up buying a 17 in. screen laptop. I thought it was huge, since I prefer lightweight computers that are easier to carry.

The one thing on Gabe's mind on that last visit was getting out. He'd be discharged the next summer. He had a hundred ideas of where he was going to live and what he'd do when he was finally home again. I think it's what kept him going through the horrors of Afghanistan. He never told me much about what he was going through, most of which was classified, but one day he did tell me he might have killed someone. They had a skirmish with the "enemy" and everyone was shooting. No one in their unit knew which bullets hit their target, but when it was over three of the Afghan soldiers were dead. The one thing he did say a lot was that he hated it.

One of his ideas was to be a CHP (California Highway Patrol). He was anxious to get started as soon as he got out, so we went over the CHP offices and talked to an officer. They told him that everyone has to go through the application process and then go to the CHP Academy, but being ex-military is a big plus. He also suggested that Gabe take a course on his own in race car driving. This really appealed to Gabe. His car was a Mazda RX8 and he always referred to it as a race car.

On his last day I took him back to the airport. I told him how much I loved being in Mexico. I lived with Roberto and we were happy together, considering each other as life partners. Gabe told me he didn't see it lasting. I blew it off. He always thought he knew everything and that he was right. Roberto broke up with me a month later.

I didn't want to let him get on the plane. We hugged and said we loved each other. I wish I could remember every word he said. I didn't know it would be the last time I'd see him alive.

CHAPTER 24:

Feelings of Guilt

WRITING MY BOOK WAS STIRRING FEELINGS I'd buried deep, helping me understand and feel the feelings I didn't even know were there. It's no wonder I'd been stuck.

I was in Nevada City in June 2016, working on my insurance audits, when our country got news of another mass shooting in Orlando, Florida. This one at Pulse, a gay nightclub. For most of us it hit hard. I wish it could awaken levels of understanding and compassion for people across the country and around the world. Yet the shootings and the hate crimes seem to keep escalating. This wasn't the first or the last. The report said a lone shooter left 49 people dead and 53 wounded.

There is one story that spoke to me personally. It was about a mother who was visiting her son. She went with him to Pulse that night, to the nightclub. They wanted to have a good time together. This was a mother that was proud of her son. She saw the shooter with his gun pointed at her son and reacted before others were aware of his malicious intent. She moved in front of him, perhaps by instinct, definitely from her love, to protect him. She ended up taking the bullet. And she died as a result.

I read this story and I cried, my heart aching for her son and their family. But I asked myself, *What was special about this story? Why was it speaking to me?*

That night I meditated to get to the root of my pain, using the meditation for holding myself in love and compassion. I asked to go to deeper levels, to find what was blocking my healing. It quickly came to me that I was holding on to guilt that my son had died, guilt that I couldn't protect him and keep him safe. My instinct as a mother was the same as that mother in the story. Like a mother bear, I'm hardwired to do anything and everything I can to protect my children.

As my kids grew into adulthood, I knew it wasn't possible to be there and to protect them in all ways. I can't keep them home with me. It's not even what they need. But it doesn't change the feeling inside of me that it is my basic nature, my deep-rooted need to protect my children.

On an intellectual level, I could look at these concepts and reason them away. It's easy to tell myself that I shouldn't feel guilty over my son's death. I wasn't even in the same country. I wasn't the one who chose for him to go in the Army and I tried talking him out of it. As a concept, I knew wasn't my fault.

But my soul and my heart didn't hear the intellectual arguments or care much for them. My heart needed to heal on the level of where it hurt. I hadn't realized I was even holding on to this guilt until I read the Orlando story, combined with my meditation to go within. Because intellectually I already knew it wasn't my fault.

My heart needed another level of healing. I felt Gabe with me in my meditation. I felt him holding me so that I could let go of the guilt. I felt him smiling at me, loving me, and wanting me to be happy.

I held myself in that feeling, us embracing each other in our mutual love. My love and connection with Gabe was so present and so strong. And my heart melted and opened.

That night I slept better than I had in a long time. Something shifted on a deep and profound level, one more layer revealed.

CHAPTER 25:

Learning to Ski and Snowboard

LIVING IN THE MOUNTAINS seemed to bring back even more memories. Maybe it was because I was writing and more focused. And maybe it was remembering those special times we'd gone to the mountains together.

One weekend, when Gabe was about 14-15 I took him on a spontaneous weekend trip to a campground in the high Sierras. It was just Gabe and me. His sisters were busy with their lives. It was mid-September and a last chance getaway before it got too cold. I let him use my old scout backpack to gather his things. It wasn't until we got there I found the backpack, that he had loaded in the car, was empty. He only had the clothes on his back. I fondly remember these silly things, how we argued over which campsite to take in an almost empty campground. We had a fire at night and shared a tent. He still liked camping and roughing it back then. I think Afghanistan (at least temporarily) cured him of that.

Now I was coming back to my home in the Sierras every summer. It was incredible. One August weekend I went with some friends on a trip to Lake Tahoe. This is where I learned to ski. Gabe learned to snowboard. This was our place.

I didn't learn to ski until I was 32. Gabe was 16. I should have learned sooner. I grew up in Utah where they have some of the best skiing in the world. But ski slopes weren't for me in those days. I was the second oldest in a family of eight kids and there was never enough money to go around. We were lucky to get a few outfits for school each year. Having money for luxuries like skiing was out of the question.

I tried it once when I was about twenty-three. I had three little kids back at home and a boyfriend that loved to ski. I think Dave grew up with skis on his feet, he'd been doing it since he was old enough to walk. He'd tell me "Skiing's better than sex!"

Dave used to take me along on his ski trips to Deer Valley. But I still didn't ski. I'd enjoy the sun, glittering off the snowy slopes, sitting in the lodge. It was a nice break from the kids, but I couldn't help but feel like I was missing out.

Everyone looked like they were having such a good time. I wanted to see those mountains from the top of the lift. But, I think I was letting myself be ruled by my own limitations and fears.

One day Dave convinced me to give it a try. He took me to Brighton, the ski resort at the top of Big Cottonwood Canyon with Mount Majestic as a backdrop. I knew these mountains. I'd grown up here. As a Girl Scout I'd hiked to the top of Mount Majestic just to see the sun rise. That was back in my high school days.

Dave insisted that there was no need to take lessons. He'd been skiing since he was three years old. It was second nature to him. He said the lessons would just slow me down. He helped me rent my equipment, showed me how to put on my boots and click in the skis. I stood up and fell down. I didn't know how to move.

Dave helped me to the lift and somehow I climbed aboard. We went up the "easy" bunny slope. I have no idea how high or steep it was, but to my inexperienced eye it grew in proportion.

I immediately fell, trying to get off the lift. Dave took me down the first time. He held me in front of him as he skied down the mountain. It was not fun! I didn't learn anything by being carried down the hill. I wasn't ready to ski on my own, but almost anything was better than that.

He took me up again and told me I had to "just do it".

"The best way to learn it to just go for it." he said. I think he gave me a few pointers. Nothing I can remember.

Dave said; "You don't need to do the pizza pie wedge, that really isn't the way to stop."

The wedge shape is something they teach you when you're learning. It's the most basic way to get yourself to stop. Stopping and turning are the most important things they teach when learning to ski. Without knowing stopping and turning there is no control.

But there I was at the top of the lift. Before Dave took off he told me to point the skis downward. So I did.

That one trip down the bunny slope seemed endless. I'd point my skis down, start going a little and then I'd freak out. I was zig-zagging, like Dave said, but that got me headed towards a bunch of trees, or off the side of the slope and into the powder, and I'd panic.

The only way to stop was to fall. I remember falling on my face, goggles planted in the snow. I'd get myself back up, point the skis back to the slope and go at it again. Fall again, up again, turn and go. By the time I made it to the bottom I was done. That run was my last for the day.

I didn't try skiing again for another ten years. It was an expensive sport. I was a single mom. I didn't have skiing friends and I didn't have money.

By the time I was 34 my kids were growing up. The girls were out on their own. I still had Gabe at home, but he was in high school. I had more freedom and a little more spending money. And I had a new boyfriend that loved to ski.

I met Tim when we were hiking. We were both members of the Diablo Hiking Club. We connected over our mutual passion for hiking and the outdoors. Then winter came. He had a cabin up at Kings Beach, on the shores of Lake Tahoe, and he invited me on a weekend ski trip. Time to learn the right way.

This time I was going to take lessons. My friend Mary wanted to join us. She had a story similar to my own of her first try. We decided to go together. We'd be on the same level, beginners. It would allow Tim to go have fun skiing while we were learning.

Tim made it easy for us. The cabin had plenty of room for the three of us. It was just 13 miles from one of his favorite resorts, Northstar. We lived three and a half hours away, in the Bay Area, so it worked best to stay overnight.

Our plans were made. We decided to go right after Christmas for a three-day weekend. Northstar had beginner packages. We got our ski rentals and lessons all in one. Mary and I signed up for two days of morning lessons, followed by free afternoons to practice on the slopes. The lessons made all the difference in the world. I learned how to slow down, stop and turn, all the basics that you need to feel confident enough to start a new sport.

One of the best lessons I learned applies to a multitude of situations in everyday life. They taught us that you will go where your eyes go. If you are looking at the trees, you will end up in the trees. (*Remember my first experience? That is exactly what I had done.*) So, instead of focusing on my fear of running off the slopes and into the trees, I focused my attention down the slope, where I wanted to go.

A friend referred to skiing as controlled falling. It's learning how to keep some control while you are basically falling down the icy mountain on slippery sticks under your feet. The key is learning that control.

I was scared at first. Even on the slight slope of the bunny hill, it took me a while to get up my nerve to turn my skis towards the downhill slope. And to turn there was that moment of pointing straight down before I was turned back the other way. I was so afraid of going too fast and losing control. But I also learned that turning uphill would slow me down. That helped a lot.

My turns were so klutzy. I must have looked hilarious (just like everyone else). But it didn't matter. The instructors were methodical and patient. They would go ahead of us and we would follow, mimicking their turns and moves. It made it easy for me. If they could do it, I could too. By the second day it started to get fun. I'd take the lift on my own, still on the bunny slopes, and ski down. By then I wasn't falling much at all. I was starting to see why people loved it so much.

After our two days of skiing, I learned something else about downhill skiing. I learned that it takes a lot of muscles I didn't even know I had. Downhill skiing looks easy. I didn't know it was going to be so much work. When I got back home I could barely walk up and down my own stairs.

But I was hooked. It was fun and Tim offered to take me again.

Gabe must have been about 15 or 16 at the time. He was a skateboarder and he begged me to take him snowboarding. So, the next trip we invited him along.

We got the weekend package again so Gabe and I both had morning lessons. Gabe was a beginner and I was now on level three.

After the lessons I met up with Gabe. He showed me he had some control of the board, so I suggested we go up the lift together. He balked. He didn't feel ready. But I told him to just follow me. I said, "If I can do it, you can do it."

He agreed to give it a try. We went up and he followed me down the slope. It was getting easier and easier for me. The bunny slope wasn't much of a slope any more. But for Gabe it was his first time going down on his own. He caught on quickly and though the board follows a different track than skis, he was able to follow me and increase his skill. We kept doing the runs all afternoon and by the end of the day Tim found us and we skied down to the car together.

Gabe's confidence and skill grew fast. By the next trip Gabe and I were equaling out on our lessons. In the afternoons we were close enough in ability that we could ski and snowboard the rest of the day. We were taking the blue, intermediate slopes. The lift took us to the top of the mountain where we could see the view all around. It was exhilarating. Going down the slopes with more speed was fun! It was better, by far, than driving a fast car on a curvy mountain road. I'd never done anything like it.

Northstar continued to be our favorite resort. After your fifth lesson, they let you take the lessons for free. I bought my own skis and boots, I no longer had to rent my equipment. Lesson five also graduates you to the back side, a full mile down the steep, black diamond slopes.

Gabe was ready for it. He took the black diamond lesson, already passing me by. But he didn't let it rest there, he had to encourage me to do it too, using the same words on me that I used on him, "If I can do it, you can do it."

I did. Just once. It was steep and I could barely move a muscle when I was done. But I did it.

Gabe went on with quite a passion for snowboarding and found ways to go every chance he could. He'd have been happy to live up there all season long. He bought his own board and boots. He'd go with his friends, or me, any chance he could get.

I split up with Tim, but Gabe and I continued to make trips together, just the two of us. We ventured out to other resorts. One time it was snowing all the way up to the mountains. We stopped at the first resort we came to, Soda Springs. I wanted to stay inside, but that would be a wasted day and a wasted ticket, so we ended up skiing through a blizzard. For me the freezing snow, blowing all around us, blocking my goggles so I could barely see, was hardly fun. But for Gabe it was just another challenge and he loved it.

Skiing and snowboarding was our thing. Gabe got better than me and moved on to buy his own board and go as often as he could with his friends. But for that year when he was 16 it was just him and me, it was what we did, together.

CHAPTER 26:

Gabe's Chapter is Over

IT WAS MY GRANDDAUGHTER, Aliyah's, birthday and I decided to do something different. I was visiting from the mountains and I took her to San Francisco's Haight-Ashbury District. She was turning 14 and it was time to initiate her into life in the Bay Area, just her and me, exploring the streets of San Francisco.

We walked in and out of stores, searching for just the right birthday present for her. A Tibetan store had richly colored purses, shirts and skirts. I showed her Rasputin Records, a store my daughters used to love for buying used records and CD's with their favorite music. Buffalo Exchange was another of their favorites as teens. The girls would buy 60's style dresses with paisley prints.

Aliyah wasn't sure what she wanted, maybe a purse or something to wear. We entered a headshop. As she looked around at the bongs and pipes she said, "I don't know if I should be in here."

Then we found some cool bags with Day of the Dead skulls and Tree of Life designs. We picked one out we both liked, but she wasn't sure if it was the one thing she wanted. I told her, "It's OK, I like it. I'll go ahead and buy it and if you find something you like better, I'll keep the purse."

A few stores later she found a tie-dyed sweatshirt and bought it. So, the bag was mine. I was looking at my new bag and found a tag that said Ixchel. It was probably made by a small local shop, but it was pretty cool that it was called Ixchel. Aliyah also looked cool in her new sweatshirt. We were both happy with our purchases.

I took her to a Mexican restaurant for lunch. We talked about a lot of things. When the subject of her Uncle Gabe came up she said, "I really don't remember him. I was so little when he died."

"Yes, you were pretty young. But I remember you liked him, especially on his last visit when you were three years old." I said.

"I wish I had something of his. Jesse and Quentin got some of his clothes, but I didn't get anything." Aliyah told me.

She was right. Jesse was her cousin, Quentin her brother. The boy cousins were only four months apart and three years older than Aliyah. They'd known Gabe better and as boys I guess it made sense to give them some of his stuff.

"I'm sorry. I wasn't here when Gabe's things were shipped back. I guess no one thought of you wanting anything. Let me look around. I still have some of his clothes, too." I said.

And I realized Aliyah would never know him more than those few memories of when she was little. My younger grandkids, Jordan and Gabe, were born after he died and would never know their uncle. And even the older ones like Julia, Alex, Jesse and Quentin only had sketchy memories that would continue to fade.

I thought about how Gabe's life was lived and over and they'd never know him any better. His chapter was done. Yet, we all continued to grow and experience new things. My grandkids had their entire lives ahead of them. That's when another layer of the finality of his life hit me, and I decided to call the book *"Forever 25."*

Days later, when I returned home to my trailer, I dug around through my box of old clothes. I'd already given away most of Gabe's things. I just didn't have use for t-shirts and jackets that didn't fit me, and even though they had Gabe's energy, I liked the idea of giving them away and letting that energy bring something to someone else's life.

Still, I had to have something left to give Aliyah. Then my hand landed on an army jacket, the camo-style that kids like to wear. I pulled it out, along with one of his army brown t-shirts and gave them to her the next time I saw her.

CHAPTER 27:

Gabe's Memorial Plaque

THAT NOVEMBER, EIGHT YEARS AFTER GABE DIED, the Blue Star Moms of Contra Costa County wanted to honor the local heroes with a memorial plaque at each of the local high schools. This was a big project. Each high school in the region was getting one of these plaques.

This was the first one and it was at Concord High School. They didn't have my contact info, but they wrote to Anni and told her about it, asking if we could be there, since he would be listed on it.

I was a bit surprised. Gabe didn't graduate. Instead he got a GED at 16 and he went right into Diablo Valley College. He wasn't dumb, he'd just had enough of the drama of high school and was ready to move on.

So when Anni told me about it I'd forgotten he'd even gone to Concord High. His sophomore year must have been around the time he was expecting his daughter. He was 17 when Angela was born. I guess I forgot what else he was doing at the time.

Anni said they might ask someone from our family to speak. She didn't want to, but I felt someone should, so I spent the day before writing a speech. I didn't know what to say and I didn't feel prepared, but I wanted to honor my son as much as I could.

Our whole family attended the ceremony: my daughters, my son-in-law, my grandkids. I felt odd as we walked into the space. I didn't know anyone there, but I felt like the ceremony was for Gabe and our family.

I found someone that appeared to be helping and introduced myself.

"I'm Gabe's mom." I said.

She looked at me funny.

"I'm the mother of Sgt. Gabriel Guzman. He's one of the soldiers on the plaque," I explained.

"Oh yes." she said. "We have seats for your family over here."

We followed to a row of reserved seats. Anni and Heidi sat on either side of me. Feeling a need for something to hold onto, I grabbed my daughters' hands. I saw their tears and knew they needed me as much as I needed them.

My older grandkids, Julia, Jesse, Quentin and Aliyah, were old enough to know Gabe as their uncle. But they were only 4 to 10 years old when he died. He was a distant memory and a picture on the wall. My two youngest, Jordan and Gabe, never met their uncle. They only knew him as a story of a soldier. For Jordan he was also the uncle who died the day she was born. She'd started wondering what that meant.

My eyes scanned the crowd. I knew there were two other families like ours. There were three soldiers listed on the plaque. I wanted to know these other moms. I felt a kinship. The names weren't just names, they were also someone's son.

Then I spotted a short woman with long, curly blond hair. She was sitting a row apart from us. We made eye contact as she stood and came to introduce herself. She was Joan Bekowsky, the mother of Cpl. Mick R. Bekowsky. He was the second name on the plaque, under Gabe. He died in 2004 in Iraq. Joan gave me a hug.

That's when I figured out why Gabe's name was first: the order had to be by rank. Gabe was a sergeant. I was proud that he stood above, not because he was better, but because he had pushed himself to achieve that rank.

Before the ceremony I also met Loretta Masnada and Carol Prell. These were the Blue Star moms that made this all happen. They wanted the fallen soldiers to be remembered. They picked the high schools to display these plaques to show the students what others had done before them.

There were people in uniforms. Important people like the mayor and school principal were in the audience. An older couple came to say hi. They were the owners of Ouimet Brothers Funeral Home. They remembered us, though I couldn't have picked them out. Gabe's service had been special, it drew such a crowd. I was impressed they remembered one of their many services from eight years ago and went out of their way to come to this event.

There were a lot of people who spoke. Loretta started out by telling about the project and what it meant for the soldiers, the families and the community. Her son, Tony, had attended school at Concord High. Now he was a Marine, tall and impressive in his full dress uniform. Tony came to the podium and started speaking:

"Good afternoon Ladies and Gentlemen. Thank you for coming.

As a Concord High Class of 2006 Graduate and Active Duty Marine, I am truly honored to be here.

I feel like only yesterday Mr. Paulson was giving me his "Good morning, Mr. Noble" like he knew I was up to something.

When my mom told me about her and Carol's idea to honor our fallen, I asked if I could say a few words on behalf the Concord High Alumni and Active Duty Military.

I have the privilege of working side by side with our nation's best daily, but rarely do I get the chance to recognize them like I do now.

It's easy to forget that at any given moment there are brave men and women somewhere in the world fighting for our country.

Many things can be said about these individuals who sacrifice so much: their family, friends, and even sometimes their lives.

Greater love hath no man than this, that a man lay down his life for his friends.

Sgt Gabriel Guzman, Cpl Mick Bekowsky, and PFC Scott Barnett gave their lives freely for something greater than themselves.

Nobody forced them to sign the contract,

Nobody forced them to raise their right hand,

And nobody forced them swear to defend this great country, against ALL enemies.

They were willing to lay down their lives for their country, for their brothers and sisters in arms ... and there is no higher calling than that.

I never met Sgt Guzman, Cpl Bekowsky, or PFC Barnett ... at least not in the literal sense.

I never met them, but I knew them.

I knew them because I've been where they have been, and I have done what they have done.

I was there with them, exhausted beyond words, but going out on a patrol nonetheless, because it was our duty and it needed to get done.

We sat in misery together when the heat was so overbearing it melted the soles of our boots.

We played monopoly for the hundredth time together, while eating the same MRE for 6 straight months.

They had my back every time we stepped outside the wire and when the enemy fire would start.

I was with them, half a world away ... missing our families.

We shed tears of joy when mom's month old cookies finally came in the mail. It was so hot they smelled oven fresh!

And we cried tears of sorrow ... when we honored our fallen brothers.

I have fought, sweat, laughed, and cried alongside them for the last 9 years.

I never met these brave Heroes, but they are my family, they are my brothers.

Because of men and women like them I will continue to fight, and strive to honor the legacy that they and so many others have left behind.

And it is my hope that when the students of Concord High walk past this memorial it is not to push them to join the military, but that they will find an ideal, an inner courage to be something great, just like these three men were and still are.

John F. Kennedy once said:

"In the long history of the world, only a few generations have been granted the role of defending freedom in its hour of maximum danger.

I do not shrink from this responsibility, I welcome it."

Sgt Gabriel Guzman, Cpl Mick Bekowsky, PFC Scott Barnett…

You are among the very best our society gave to keep the American dream alive.

Batman, Ironman, Superman…

Step aside, I know who my true heroes are."

He finished and I was crying. I'd never heard anything like this, his perspective as a soldier in the field. It gave me a glimpse into Gabe's army life.

Then Joan Bekowsky went to the front to speak about her son. I don't remember what she said, but she'd been through the same hurt as me. I felt her pain.

The ceremony was finally drawn to a close and the plaque revealed. They hadn't called on me or even asked if I'd like to speak. But it didn't matter. I'd heard the words of a fellow soldier and another mom. They'd spoken what I didn't know how to say.

They called us Gold Star Moms to come up to the plaque and pull back the cloth. We posed for pictures of the plaque, with the moms, then with our family. Reporters took pictures as well. It would be in the papers.

I'd already seen it in the picture we'd been sent, but I took time to read the plaque and look at the names. It reads:

CONCORD HIGH SCHOOL

Dedicated to those who died while serving
in the Iraq and Afghanistan Wars.

Sgt. Gabriel Guzman
United States Army
17 Oct 1982 - 8 Mar 2008
Operation Enduring Freedom

Cpl. Mick R. Belowsky
United States Marine Corps.
19 July 1983 - 6 Sept. 2004
Operation Iraqi Freedom
CHS Class of 2001

Pfc. Scott G. Barnett
United States Army
10 Nov. 1985 - 28 Jan. 2010
Operation Iraqi Freedom

Our Heroes Will Never Be Forgotten

The high school kids may walk past this plaque and not even notice it. Perhaps a few will. Maybe they'll even have an annual assembly to remember the soldiers. That would be nice, but probably still not hit home for a young teen.

I've walked past thousands of memorials and plaques in my life, but they were always some impersonal remembrance of the past. I see them differently now. I take a moment to slow down and read what is written. I think of the lives they represent.

We all had refreshments. The kids grew restless. It had been a lot of sitting for them. I wanted to stay and get to know the people better, but I knew the kids were pretty much done.

Then an old biker came over and introduced himself as Spike. He was one of the Patriot Guard who rode for Gabe's funeral. He'd fought in Vietnam. He took us out to see his chopper.

I asked him, "You remember Gabe's funeral?"

He said, "I remember them all. We're there every time a soldier's brought home. I remember the day they brought Gabe. It rained. At the last minute we were told we had to go to the Napa Airport instead of Concord."

I hadn't met him that day. I hadn't met any of them. But like the funeral directors, he remembered that day, not just as another day with another soldier. He remembered the details. He remembered my son.

CHAPTER 28:

We Need Our Soldiers

OVER THE YEARS SINCE GABE JOINED THE ARMY I have tried looking at the army and our soldiers from all different angles. Although I don't support the wars that they have been fighting in, I think we all want our men and our soldiers to protect us. We take for granted the fairly peaceful country that generations of soldiers have created for us.

It's easy to see the fallen hero as the ideal of this. They gave the ultimate sacrifice, they died for their country. But what kind of sacrifice was made by those who came home, what of the survivors?

I've had two psychic readings, about 3 years apart. Two different psychics channeled Gabe for me, and what came through was surprisingly consistent. There was no connection between the two ladies, but their words were almost identical. One of the things Gabe told me in these sessions was that he just couldn't take it any more, he couldn't stand being there, in Afghanistan, with the war and seeing the people and how they lived and what they went through. His spirit choose death over sticking with it and coming back home where he would have to live with all that he had been through.

Being in those conditions changes a person. The brave young man wants to prove himself. He may have his own crosses to bear and fighting in a war may even be an outlet for his inner aggression. Yet who is truly ready to fire a gun at another human being? What happens to a person who has to kill someone else, even when they have been taught that the other person is *"the enemy?"* How do they carry on when they've seen friends and comrades killed in action?

My son thought he was ready to fight for his country. He choose to go. In fact, one of his comrades told me he had willingly volunteered when he was sent on his first tour to Iraq. He was young and green and ready to see the action. But three years later, when he was sent to Afghanistan, he wasn't quite as willing; in fact he was scared. He was much more seasoned by then and had a clearer picture of what to expect.

He hated it in Afghanistan. He hated the poverty. He hated the conditions, the cold and miserable barracks. He complained about his computer that suddenly didn't want to charge any more. I remember him telling me he wanted to throw it off a bridge. Yet the computer was one of the few distractions he had from being there, and even the privilege to use it was taken away from him as punishment when he didn't do things like he was supposed to.

On his last leave stateside the only thing he could focus on was how ready he was to have it all over with and come back home. The army did everything they could to try to get him to re-enlist, but he wanted nothing to do with it. For security reasons, he couldn't tell me much of what went on over there, but there was that time he said he might have killed someone. He could never know whose bullet hit, but it could have been his and it was obvious that this bothered him.

Since Gabe's death I haven't had a chance to talk to other soldiers about their experience. I haven't been around those soldiers that came home. My life just hasn't taken that direction. But, I have met a few people who have been in wars or heard stories. It causes me to reflect on what it means to be the warrior or soldier who comes home and how that experience informs a person's life.

I have one friend that not only fought in a war, but also lost his brother. I met him when he was in a relationship that later broke up, so I knew him and the girlfriend. But with the drama of a breakup his ex-girlfriend felt it was so important to tell me that he had a terrible temper at home. The side of him that I saw has always been loving and kind. It made me wonder how difficult it was for him to work with the feelings and emotions of all that he had been through. I could not imagine what it would be like for me to live with such emotions. I can only have compassion for such a man.

George Carlin talks about PTSD in his comedy skit, where he points out the dehumanization of even the terms used for PTSD as he explains: "A condition in combat when a fighting person's nervous system is stressed to its absolute peak and maximum, can't take any more input, the nervous system is either snapped or is about to snap. In the 1st World War that condition was called *'shell shock.'* By the 2nd World War the same condition was called *'battle fatigue.'* By the war in Korea this same condition was called *'operation exhaustion.'* Then, after the war in Vietnam it was changed again to *'Post-Traumatic Stress Disorder'.*"

And as we dehumanize the words for the condition, we also dehumanize the person. They are not called soldiers or men, they are called *"troops."* I was in Girl Scouts as a kid and the word troop meant a group of us, so when I finally looked it up and found that for the Army *"troops"* meant each person it seemed a bit odd. But it is just another way to distance ourselves from the humanity of the situation.

When it comes to PTSD, it seems in our society we are quick to give the label and slap a diagnosis on it, yet distance ourselves from those who suffer from it. We tend to think of it as something they should get over, never looking deeper to understand what the person is feeling.

I have another friend whose son went to Afghanistan. When he returned home he didn't know how to process the traumatic experiences he had faced. Without support he turned to alcohol and drugs to cope. Soon he was labeled in the system for the drug and alcohol problems and his PTSD was ignored.

His story turned even more tragic one night. He'd been drinking and crashed into another car. Though he was going only 20 MPH the older man he hit wasn't wearing a seatbelt and he died. My friend's son was sentenced to 15 years in prison for manslaughter. In prison he still gets no help or support to cope with the PTSD, and added to that is the trauma of causing the death of another man. The prison scene is even worse than the war. In one week alone there were three people stabbed while standing in the chow line, leading to hospitalization. One inmate tried to escape over the barbed wire fence and was taken to the hospital for injuries incurred trying to get away. My friend's son is not a hardened criminal, yet his life after the war has gone from bad to worse.

We, as a society, expect these men, and women, to come back and fit into everyday life as if nothing had changed. We expect them to get a job and be a normal functioning person. We don't realize that everything has changed and the re-entry is not so smooth.

In my spiritual teaching I have learned to look at aspects we consider Sacred Feminine and Sacred Masculine. In this work, I've often heard women say we don't need any more *"the Masculine."* They fed up with patriarchy. I disagree, we need men and women, we need masculine and feminine. I believe we can never be balanced if we don't have both.

I've studied and put a lot of thought into what it is that distinguishes something as *"sacred."* What is feminine and what is sacred feminine? What is masculine and what makes it sacred masculine? We all have both feminine and masculine traits, and most people have more of one than the other (regardless of which sex their body is). It's innate to our nature. And those feminine or masculine traits can express in lower ways of being or they can express in a higher, more enlightened or conscious way. It is the way those traits are expressed that would make them more sacred.

For example, feminine traits include connectedness, community, intuitiveness. Women have the ability to create life from the darkness of the womb. They hold the unlimited potential for life to bring forth its own divine expression. Their energy is like a web, as they have an innate awareness of all those in their care, such as their husband and children. It is natural for women to *"multitask"* since their awareness stretches out to all that is in their surroundings. Yet those same qualities that make them good at taking care of their families can be harmful and destructive when this connectedness turns to gossiping about everyone in their community. Other negative expressions of the feminine include cattiness and witchiness. Women have a very strong innate power, and just as the Goddesses of Creativity (in their many forms) can call the storms, they can be destructive in their wrath. So, it is the awareness of the feminine power and a choice to use it in a good way that brings it to the *"sacred."*

The same is true with the masculine. We are used to seeing the abuse of masculine power. We see it as controlling and egocentric. We see men blindly charging into a fight or war. There are many ways that misuse of this energy has hurt our planet. Yet on the flip side of this there are wonderful traits that the masculine represents. It is in their nature to protect their families and communities. They are the natural providers. Their quick action and single-mindedness can be very direct and bring to life ideas and plans. They often bring a strength that helps carry us through difficult times.

I love seeing men in their power in a positive way. They are the natural warriors. And when I'm in danger I want to have a strong man on my side. We do need our warriors.

I think it's time we also recognize what these men do for us, whether off at war or on the home front. I think it's time for us to open our hearts to our returning soldiers and have empathy for their struggles. Recognize that war has changed them and help them find their way back to their selves, to be the men they truly wish to be.

CHAPTER 29:

Ideas for Ritual

MY NEW MOUNTAIN HOME was only a mile and a half walk into downtown Nevada City, but it felt quiet and remote. There were no houses on the side of my RV. Out my front door all I saw were tall pines. The opposite side was up against an old shack and to the back was a tree-covered slope down to an open meadow of our closest neighbors, a wedding center. But we rarely saw them, as they only had weddings there on warm summer evenings.

It was idyllic. But the next summer I came back from my winter in Mexico to find out they were putting in a campground across the street. The InnTown Campground would have overnight camping, RV spots, and glamping tents. I wasn't sure if that was such a great idea.

The open lot had been developed. I could see a gate going in and a main building. They were opening July 4th, so I figured I better check it out. My landlady, Vicky, also told me they were connecting a back trail into town. I did like that, I loved walking into town.

One day I decided to see what was going on and explore the new trail. I walked into the campground, passed where they were installing a front gate. I used to be able to walk right through here, without bothering anyone. It was so different now, and actually it was quite impressive.

The manager, Jed, came and introduced himself. It was his job to know who was on the property. I told him I lived across the street and wanted to see the place. He showed me the main building with a small store. He took me around to see the campsites and glamping tents. The tents were pretty sweet. They were fixed tents on platforms and each had a double bed. The owner had decorated each unit in different colors with a rustic, framed picture and old-fashioned quilt. Out the back were balconies and guests had use of propane campfires.

The property had remnants of its former life, from when the narrow gauge railroad came through. There was the false front of an old western town and saloon. They planned to use this area to show movies at night for the kids. Next to it was the old Chinese Cemetery. This was an actual cemetery for the Chinese people who had worked in the gold mines, but the gravestones had been lost and it was in disrepair. The InnTown Campground was working with the Chinese Historical Society to repair the gravesites. On the backside were further remains of the old Northern Queen Railroad, with parts of the track and one of the old rail cars.

Jed left me on my own to wander around and explore. I could see a sign for hikers pointing to a small covered bridge that led into an abandoned park. This was the trail into town.

I decided to save that for another day and headed back. As I came to the front gate there was a tiny house for the new night host. I could see him tinkering around his yard area and when I came close he introduced himself as Scott. He had just moved in the month before. Scott was friendly and invited me to check out his new tiny house. He had a small dog that looked like Toto, but his name was Dante. Scott was grilling buffalo burgers and asked me to stay for dinner. We talked for hours, getting to know each other. We had a lot in common. He liked hiking and holding ceremony. I went home excited to have a friend and neighbor to hang out with.

After that Scott and I got together once or twice a week. We'd take Dante for walks in the woods, along canal trails, or walk into town. Sometimes I'd come over and join him on his evening rounds. He'd moved here from Arcata and was recently divorced. But his ex now lived up the street from us and they were still good friends.

For over 20 years Scott had been a psychiatrist. He also practiced shamanism and had formed groups in Arcata. He wanted to do something like that in Nevada City. He thought of opening a practice called Shamanic

Psychotherapy. I told him it would be a great idea. Combining the two fields seemed a perfect fit.

Over time I shared parts of my story about Gabe. He had a son named Gabe as well. Then he told me he'd studied with Malidoma Patrice Some and learned his version of grieving rituals. I told him how much I wanted to do a grieving ritual and maybe we could even organize group rituals I could do with him. We started talking about ideas for working together and creating a weekend ritual event.

Our thoughts flowed as we got to know each other, talking as we explored the local trails. But eventually I realized his ideas and mine didn't quite match up.

He said, "A grieving ritual is for anyone and everyone. We all experience grief, especially with all the terrible things happening in the world."

"Yes," I said. "But there is a different level of grief of a child or family member or someone close to you. This is a very specific grief and one that takes on a deeper level of understanding and healing. I want to work on this level of grief, because that's the level I'm working through myself."

We talked about it more, but we never got closer to agreeing. My calling wasn't the same as his. But by then my desire for grieving ritual had grown. .

I thought about it more. I considered taking a course or class, perhaps one with Malidoma. I saw other classes online about Grief and Death, but they still didn't fit what I knew as my way and my truth.

I was ready to connect more with other mothers, fathers, families. I started noticing more when people on Facebook posted photos or told of a death in their family. I was talking about my son more, and I seemed to be meeting more people in real life with similar experiences as well.

I met a friend, Victoria, on Facebook who had also lost her son. She took this work seriously. She was creating a documentary about grief.

Victoria posted pictures of a grieving ritual they did for their young family. They honored her son's death with ritual every year in a Day of the Dead ceremony. Then I noticed I was jealous, because I'd never known how to do something like this and felt I had "done it wrong" to not know how to honor my son this way. Then I realized how ridiculous it was to think I could do it wrong or to be jealous of how someone else grieves. Her pain was no less than mine and her way of dealing with it not better or worse than mine. Still, I liked the idea of a ritual.

Even though I had lived in Mexico off and on for almost 10 years, I still didn't really understand the Day of the Dead. It wasn't my culture and I didn't know how to connect to it. Then the movie *"The Book of Life"* came out, followed a few years later by *"Coco."* These movies helped me understand Day of the Dead and the honoring of our ancestors better than I had from living in Mexico.

I still felt like an outsider, trying to find my way to grieve. I wanted a ritual that fit for me.

CHAPTER 30:

Memories: Who Was Gabe?

SOMETIMES MOVIES HELP get in touch with my feelings. Other movies I will never see, like the movie *"Stop Loss"* that came out the same year Gabe died. It hit too close to home. Yet, *"Charlie Wilson's War"* helped me to see more of what the war in Afghanistan was about and even though I cried, I was glad I watched it.

When I watched the movie *"Saint Vincent"* it helped me see why the phrase "sorry for your loss" never felt good. It's a 2014 film with Bill Murray. The story is about a young kid who befriends a crotchety older man. I love these kind of movies, about seeing the good in another person.

There is a part in the movie where the kid (Oliver) is asking the Bill Murray character (Vincent or Vin) about his wife who had passed on.

Here's the interchange:

Oliver: Sorry, Vin, for your loss.

Vincent: Never understood... wh-wh-why people say that.

Oliver: They don't know what else to say.

Vincent: How about, "What was she like?" "Do you miss her?" Or "What are you gonna do now?"

I think that's what's missing. It's why those words always felt so hollow to me. Watching the movie helped me put my finger on it.

I don't think anyone has ever asked me those questions. In all the years of me telling people I've lost my son, no one ever asked me about him.

How do I answer those questions? Who was my son?

Gabe was a handsome young man (yes, I'm his mom and all moms say that about their kids). But looking back at some of his pictures, I think he could have modeled for GQ. He's got a photo where he looks like that's what he was doing.

Gabe wasn't tall, but he made up for it by bodybuilding and strength training. Growing up he was a fan of Bruce Lee and wanted to practice martial arts. Unfortunately, I couldn't afford Karate classes, but he got lucky for a while and the mom of Sean, his best friend, covered the fees so he could learn. That didn't last long, but the dream never died. When he got older he enrolled himself in USKO in Concord and went all the way to Black Belt.

Was he always a warrior, like he said? Maybe he was. He loved Power Rangers and Ninja Turtles and later on Mortal Kombat. There was the year I made him a Ninja Warrior costume, yellow and black, for Halloween.

Another of his heroes was Arnold Swartzenegger, I think because he promoted fitness. Gabe pushed himself to be his best, continuing his workouts even in Afghanistan. He had me order and ship protein supplements to him, wherever he was.

His roommate from Ft. Bragg wrote me:

"All three of us, Gabe, Mike, and myself, were fitness junkies. It's amazing how we burnt our youth in service. Even after the rolling hours of training and everything, if we got off work to go home to our apartment we would put on our bulletproof vests for added weight and still go running at night together or we would be in the gym. Gabe was really skilled at wrestling and combatives, I boxed."

One of his friends and comrades from Afghanistan told me:

"We had Madden tournaments every Sunday and all the guys would get together and play. Gabe was ALWAYS my kryptonite! He beat me almost every time. I beat others soundly and the ones I beat could beat him, but his butt would kill me!"

Gabe, himself, would talk about it a lot. He'd tell me that his strength and physical condition were more mental training than anything. I was pretty focused on diet and believed food was more important and I suggested he eat better. But he told me the military rations were far from being nutritious; they seemed to be the bare minimum to keep them going. He came to believe that regardless of our health craze in the US and all the focus on eating just the right thing, what he ate had very little to do with his overall health in the end. He also pointed out that the big, tough-looking guys would cave under pressures of their training and the stress of Army life. Those that did best were the men with strong minds. He felt his smaller stature and quick intelligence helped him to excel. And he seemed to prove himself in many ways throughout his military career.

His astrological sign was Libra. Gabe certainly demonstrated Libra traits to a T. His sense of balance and fairness had him arguing all sides of an issue, every time. Whatever I was talking about or explaining, he would argue for the opposite. I hated the arguing and didn't realize until much later that's just how he was. My grandson, Jesse, is a fellow Libra. He does the same thing.

Gabe was also highly intelligent and he loved to read. He acted as if he was above other people, as if he just knew more and knew what was right and wrong. He'd say, "Don't ever doubt me," always with a bit of humor and arrogance mixed together. Yet, for all his superiority, far too often he was right. He had a great heart and I couldn't help but love him.

Always the warrior, Gabe would protect his friends and family from harm. After his death I would often hear stories of how he came to the defense of someone in need. He would always encourage his family and friends to be their best and find their inner strength.

He was a good and easy kid, until his teenage years when a bit of natural rebellion set in. He had two older sisters who helped shape and mold him, but he was always his own person. He'd play along with them, as it suited him, and then go his own way. He was always a bit of a loner, but like me, he had a few really close friends. He didn't seem to need or want to follow any crowds or try to change who he was to fit in.

When he was a young teen he saw his big sisters getting into trouble and wanted to assure me he'd never worry me like they did or do what they did. Of course, when he got a few years older he still had his turn to act out, like cutting school and getting bad grades. His daughter, Angela, was born when he was sixteen or seventeen.

And even though Angela had Down Syndrome, it never bothered him. He loved her so much. He'd do almost anything for her. He always made sure to visit and spend time with her every time he came home on leave. He'd be there for her birthdays. Back at barracks he'd show her picture around and keep it close to his heart.

Even though he was way off in Afghanistan, I really couldn't imagine a life without him. It still boggles my mind. I wonder how life can just keep going on with Gabe not part of it.

Now I like to think of Gabe as my cheerleader or fan, up there in heaven, rooting for me and wanting me to be my best. Maybe he's even pulling a few strings to smooth the way or make things easier for me. After he died, it was the first time I wasn't afraid of death. I knew he'd be there greeting me when I got there.

I think of how Gabe was so focused on health and physical strength and I use that to encourage and push myself. I'd like to make him proud. If there is anyone that inspires me more than I do for myself, it's him. I want more than a boring and normal life, I want to make this world a better place.

I'd like this book to inspire others, in some way, to find a better way of being. I want us to find solutions to conflicts rather than fighting and war. I think we can be better people together, more tolerant and cooperative. After so many thousands of years on this planet, we should be able to find a better way.

Gabe was an important part of my life and other people's lives as well. I know of at least six people who named their baby after him, a couple even before he died. He made an impact. I believe Gabe brought something to this world that is beyond just the span of the life he lived.

PART 4

CHAPTER 31:

Saying Goodbye to California

IN SEPTEMBER 2017 IT WAS TIME AGAIN FOR A
CHANGE. I was saying goodbye to California. I felt a sense
of melancholy, mixed with a need to let go. My family is in
California: my two daughters and Amy, my daughter-in-
love (a term I use for a relative that came into the family
through relationship – in this case Gabe's ex and the mother
of my granddaughter – because our relationship is not about
legal responsibility, it's about love). All of my grandchildren
are there, all within a 10 mile radius, and since I'm a gypsy
that lives part of the year in Mexico, I miss out on a lot by
not being around more as they grow up.

Our family has been in California for a long time. I
moved us there in 1991 as my oldest daughter was just
starting middle school. That was back when I was working

as an insurance auditor and the company I worked for promoted me with a relocation to California. I was taking over as the new audit manager. At 32 years old it was my first chance to be in a management position and it was a great opportunity.

I took Gabe with me on that first trip down there to find us a house. He was nine years old at the time and it was fun having him along. I enjoy the company of my kids. The trip was like a vacation, just him and me. We played games on the flight down. We shared a hotel room, paid for by the company, and he helped me pick out a house. Money had always been so tight for me and we couldn't afford real vacations, so it was nice to stay in a hotel and have someone else pick up the tab.

California was a new land to be discovered. We had been living in Seattle for the past year. I enjoyed Seattle, but I didn't realize how the heavy, dark skies and drizzly rain had affected me. It was February when we first came to California, a cold time of the year, but we arrived to clear blue skies and moderate temperatures. I felt myself thawing out and relaxing into the warmer weather. And my mind opened to the expanse of open skies. I appreciated the soft rolling hills that contrasted the dark evergreens covering Washington's west coast. As beautiful as they were, I hadn't realized how enclosed the gray skies and tall trees had made me feel.

Gabe and I quickly found a three-bedroom house on a golf course community in Livermore and came back to pack and move. We settled in for a year at that house. But my work took me all over the Bay Area, and our company office was in Concord, about an hour from our home. The late nights of reviewing other auditors' work got me home that much later. So, once our lease was up, we moved to Concord so I could be closer to the office. I always had a restless spirit and never felt quite at home anywhere. I continued to move our family, as often as once a year, but I pretty much stayed in the Concord and Martinez area until the kids were out of school and on their own.

Looking back at those years, I realize I was always part gypsy. I wanted a good home for my family, but at that point in my life I was so caught up with working and raising my family that I didn't really know myself or how much I needed movement. Without a real opportunity to travel I think I expressed it by moving our home.

Throughout their middle school to high school years we lived in various places in Concord and Martinez. When Gabe was in high school and his sisters were already living on their own, his girlfriend, Amy got pregnant and soon they moved out. With a newfound freedom, I started to follow my own dreams.

I moved to Ashland, Oregon and then to Northern California. From there, my next adventure took me to Mexico. Our family was scattered as well. Gabe was in the Army, Heidi had been living in Mount Shasta, Anni was in Sacramento. We were all individually finding our way through life. But that changed when Gabe died. Somehow, his death brought us all back to the Concord area again. We'd had his funeral there, where his childhood friends could show their respect. Soon after, Anni decided to move back and buy a house there, and Heidi followed to be closer to her sister. I came back from Mexico that fall for the visit that kept me there for two years.

That time together was important. We all needed each other as we maneuvered our way through our grief.

But now, almost ten years later, it was time to move on. I still loved my trailer in the mountains. The kids would visit in the summer and we'd go out to the Yuba River for the day or paddleboarding on Scott Flat Reservoir. Then we'd walk into town and eat at Lefty's, a great hamburger and sandwich restaurant along the river.

So it wasn't easy to move away, but it had been stewing in me for a while that something needed to change. If I kept up with insurance auditing I'd never be any happier or get any further ahead. I was more stuck than ever.

I started feeling it that spring, the need for change brewing inside me. I was in Tlayacapan, Mexico, where I rented a two-bedroom home for somewhere between $150-$170 a month, depending on the currency conversion rates. The price was right, but it didn't feel like a home.

I was getting ready to return to the states and started thinking that there must be a better way to make life in the states work for me. I was paying almost three times my Mexico rent just for space to live on with my RV and I was also paying a payment on the trailer itself. I was working more just to pay for something I only partly used. I had played with ideas of buying my own land in the area. But feeling so unhappy with enslaving myself to my work, I even thought of just selling the RV and having no home in the US.

I decided to get out of the box of my own head and past my limited thinking by turning it over to the Universe for help. The next morning I had an offer from a friend in Colorado to go live there and work with her and her family at a retreat center they had there. It felt like an answered prayer. They needed help and I loved that kind of atmosphere. I had just been thinking about how happy I was when I lived at the retreat center in Mexico the first few years I was there. It was definitely a big change, out of the box. But the idea of leaving California was difficult and in the end it didn't work out. It didn't offer a solution to the money issues, I'd still have to do the insurance work, plus the extra work of helping the retreat center.

So, I settled into being back in California for the summer and enjoying the closeness of my family. I had each of my two youngest grandkids come spend a week with me and we got to do some one-on-one grandma/grandkid time.

By the end of the summer, those nagging feelings surfaced again. I was getting ready to return to Mexico and I felt I needed to do something, not to just keep paying the rent when I wasn't there. This time an even more out-of-the box solution appeared. I was talking to my ex-brother-in-law, Dennis, who lives in Arizona. He runs Airbnb rooms out of his large home and does quite well. It's given him enough income to pay his house payments and get by, cutting back on the handyman work he had been making a living at. He suggested we move my RV there and rent it out when I'm not around. It would save me rent and also pay enough for the monthly payment. During busy months it would even make money, which we agreed to split half and half. We decided to give it a try.

The month of August went by quickly as I got things ready and he came up to help me. Dennis had a cargo van that was big enough to tow my trailer and by the end of the month we pulled out on a two-day road trip to take it to its new home. (This was the first time I'd moved it since I bought it a couple of years ago. Even though it's a trailer, I didn't buy it to travel in, just to live in.)

Dennis and I (well, mostly him) spent the next couple of weeks getting the space and the interior ready for guests. I had to put a lot of stuff in bins in the garage. The RV is fairly new, and at 31 ft. long with a slide out, it's roomy and clean. Dennis added a patio out front. The first guest booked before I even left and it kept steadily full all through the busy seasons. The people loved the environment, more like glamping than a regular house stay. They got their own kitchen, bathrooms and fully private space. And the reviews were great, carrying over from the Super Host status that Dennis had already earned. He's friendly and engaged with his guests and it really makes a difference.

The first thing I did was quit the insurance job altogether. I felt a relief I hadn't felt in years. I'd have to sort out how to split my time in the US between Arizona and California. Making this choice felt good at first, but it still felt a bit like I was abandoning my family. I'd have to decide if I was going to stay in my RV when I came back or hang out on my daughter's sofa. I had created a hole for myself, where I had retreated inward, and it was time to find my way back out.

CHAPTER 32:

A New Chapter

GABE'S LIFE WAS OVER, but there were new chapters for the rest of us. Gabe would be turning 36 years old as his daughter, Angela, just turned 18.

This year was a big year in Angela's life. She graduated from high school in June. She went to a mainstream high school and she received a special award in her special ed class. She was there with her mom, her step-dad and her new little brother. She'd been so happy when her mom married Brad. She felt like she was getting married. And her brother Garret was already a year old at her graduation. Of course he was a bit bored, but she loves having a brother. She helps mom out and plays with him all the time.

But this is one of the things Gabe isn't there for. It's times like this I miss him so much, realizing all that he is missing out on with her. As usual, I cried to see my granddaugther growing up and graduating, but thinking of Gabe and knowing he wasn't there to see his daughter, I cried even more.

Her 18th birthday was in August. Such a big milestone. She started Adult Ed where they teach her living skills. She's got a job in the back room at TJ Maxx. She's a happy and helpful kid.

I think of all she's missing by not having him there. Amy tells me she loves to see pictures of her daddy and she's got her own album that she'll just go into her room and look through. I'm glad to hear that. It's so hard to know how much a girl with Down Syndrome understands, so I'm glad to know she knows who her real daddy is.

CHAPTER 33:

Feeling into my Womb

MY LIFE STARTED A NEW CHAPTER AS WELL, one of reconnecting. I decided to retake the Women's Ceremony class again, with my teacher, Teri, and got many unexpected and powerful gifts …

In this work with the Sacred Feminine we talk about the womb and do meditation on holding ourselves within the loving space of the womb. It's a strange topic for many people. Other than for health reasons, we rarely mention it or think about it in our society. But for me I have a very different experience. I'd been doing these ceremonies and meditations for many years and it had become common practice for me to connect to the womb.

So, as part of this new class, we were guided into the meditation of holding ourselves in the womb. Even though

I'd been through this meditation so many times, this time it took me to feelings I hadn't experienced before. Usually I feel myself being held in this vague, dark place of the womb. This time I felt more deeply connected to my physical womb and to its memories. The meditation took me back to feeling the life inside me when I was holding my babies as they grew in me. It brought tears streaming down my cheeks with the depth of love the memories brought.

I felt all three of my children and the beauty of the lives created through me, sensing the life they were each born to live. I saw them grow and become the unique individuals that they were. I watched as they grew through childhood to adulthood and went out into the world. I felt that each person they touched and each life they affected was connected back to me, that through me each one of them affected the world.

I felt the potential life of each of my grandchildren being held in my womb as well, that each of their lives also came into being through me.

I was aware that the day was Veteran's Day and my awareness drifted to my son. I saw the people whose lives he'd touched and the friends he had made. I saw how he influenced these people with words of love and support. I felt and saw the difference he made in their lives in ways that continue, even though he is gone. I felt the difference he made in my life.

And I felt not only the gift of bringing all these lives into the world, but also the gift back to me, in all I have received as a mother and grandmother. Such is the circle of life and I am grateful for my part in it.

CHAPTER 34:

My Women's Initiation

TERI TAUGHT ME *"you can tell that a ceremony will be powerful by what challenges you face in getting there."* This was never more true for me than when I attended my Women's Initiation Ceremony in August of 2018.

I wasn't even planning on going, but at the same time I had been allowing for the possibility of it. If it was meant to happen, things would magically open for me to be there.

For an entire year I had been apprenticing with a group of women to become keepers of an ancient ceremony for women, focused around the womb, water and the full moon.

The invitation came in October, from my teacher Teri, in an email, to women feeling called to learn and become keepers of the ceremony. I felt a pull. I was already a full-fledged keeper of this ceremony, but I hadn't been holding my own ceremonies for years. I felt lost and disconnected. Perhaps retaking the lessons would bring me back.

I was accepted within the group. Everyone else was new. Though this apprenticeship program had been offered for over 10 years and we already had about 30 or more apprenticed keepers, I was the first one to ever ask to take it over again. But it felt good to be part of the program and getting to know the new women.

From November through December we attended weekly meetings, going through the steps of what ceremony is, elements of ceremony, different types of ceremony and how to connect with the spirits and hold ceremonies.

In January we moved on to monthly meetings and went deeper into our teaching, Teri's work with the meditations had evolved and she taught us more of what she had learned. This time we focused more on holding space, a practice of holding that simply holds ourselves and others as we are. Similar to a seed in the earth or a child in the womb, the true nature of the seed will emerge in its own way when simply nurtured.

In holding we give that energy of love and compassion and nurturing to what we are holding. We begin with holding ourselves. I was very good at holding space for others, it was an extension of what I had learned years ago on my trip to Medjurgore with James Twyman, "seeing as God sees." What I needed to practice was holding myself. Teri emphasized how important it is to hold ourselves first, before we can hold anyone else.

Teri led us in deep meditations together, going into the womb and holding ourselves in various ways, through our challenges, or hurts, and our deepest desires. As a group we participated in the women's ceremonies and held ceremonies of our own. We'd meet together each month and share our stories in deep and meaningful talking circles.

Our first class in November was with 11 women. Over the months the numbers dwindled. I guess this was normal. I felt connected to everyone in the class and was sad to see them go. One reason I was retaking this class was to connect with the community of women and I wanted to see the group continue to grow and evolve into something more.

The apprenticeship was a total of nine months, the same amount of time for a baby to grow in the womb. We were going through our own gestation and birthing. I knew this from my first apprenticeship. There were powerful changes going on inside of me beyond my conscious awareness.

By June our class meetings were coming to a completion. It was time to prepare and register for our initiation ceremony in New Mexico. We were given the option to attend in-person or via Zoom calls from home, but in order to complete our apprenticeship we were required to attend.

I figured I'd probably do the Zoom call. I couldn't really afford the in person retreat. Though the costs were kept low, I just didn't have the money. If Spirit wanted me to be there, I'd find a way, but it didn't feel as important to be there live since I'd been initiated 10 years prior.

There were preparations for us to complete for our initiation. I wasn't taking them seriously, either. Each woman was asked to make her own sacred objects to use in her ceremonies. This consisted of a water bowl, a talking stick and a ceremonial dress. We were instructed in how to treat our ceremonial objects, but we could be unique in expressing our own personality in creating them.

Yet, with the onset of summer and the winding down of our classes, I got busy and distracted with everyday life. I was visiting my family in California and the practice of ceremony was forgotten. Not being in my own place, I had no 'sacred space' to retreat to or quiet time away from everyone.

I wanted to be there. I love retreats and being together with 'sisters' of the ceremony. I knew if I went to the retreat I would be reconnected and pulled back in, I just didn't see how I could afford to go.

Then, pieces of the puzzle started to fall into place. Originally, I thought I was going to be in Mexico when they held the retreat, but at the end of March I got news that my 84-year-old mom was in the hospital and it seemed pretty serious. She was in a lot of pain, but it took them a week to diagnose that she had appendicitis.

My plans changed. I had been putting off visiting my mom, figuring there was always time. Her illness shocked me into realizing this might not be true. She was getting older.

I called my daughters to give them the news about their grandma. Anni asked if I was going to go see her. I hadn't thought about it, but I knew it would be a good idea. I might be running out of time. Even if she recovered, which I hoped she would, I did want to spend time with her while she was still healthy enough to know me, and for us both to enjoy our time together.

She was living with my youngest brother, Derek. I called and asked him if he thought I should come. He seemed relieved and quickly invited me to stay in a spare room. He was feeling quite overwhelmed with trying to take care of everything going on with Mom, as well as his own little family. He had a new eight-month-old daughter and he worked from home, so taking care of her and trying to get his work done were keeping him busy without anything extra. I got excited to meet my new niece and I told him I'd be happy to help with her as well. My grandkids were all growing up and I was missing babies.

My time is pretty flexible, since I'm a freelancer and what they call 'location independent', so I decided to go for a couple of months, planning to return to Mexico in June. I had to fit in a quick trip to California the first week of June to see my grandkids, Quentin and Angela, graduate from high school. Graduations are one of those important life events to me. They are worth some extra effort for me to attend.

But I ended up staying longer again. My daughter, Anni, asked if I could stay with her family for the summer and help with watching her daughter. Summers are hard for her as a single and working mom. Really, I loved being there for the summer. It gave me an excuse to be with my kids and grandkids while they were out of school.

The retreat seemed more possible as I checked the calendar. I found that the kids would go back to school just days before the retreat began, so the timing would work out perfectly for me to attend. I could fly to New Mexico as a stop on my way back home to Mexico.

I still didn't plan to go or buy the plane ticket. There were a lot of costs involved and after being in the US for five months, I was quickly running out of money. I can afford my simple life because I live in Mexico where so many things are cheaper. But I was getting to the point where I needed to get back there and let my finances balance out again.

It was getting near the end of June and I was going to have to decide soon. Teri sent an email that there were some funds available for partial scholarships and to write if you wanted to apply. They would send an application.

I wrote back that I'd like an application, though I was so low on funds that I wouldn't be able to go if only part of it was paid. I didn't want to take the funds if someone else needed them. I'd been through it before. I wanted to give someone else a chance. So I didn't even turn in the application.

A week or two later Teri emailed to tell me they had decided to award a full scholarship for me, to cover my plane ticket and retreat costs. After all the volunteer work I'd done for the organization, it was justified. I felt so happy. I realized that God/Spirit must want me to be there, and that felt good on so many levels, like I was an important part of the grand plan and God or Spirit was supporting me.

After a few months of neglect, it also reminded me to get back into the energy and preparing for the ceremony. I had ceremonial items from my first initiation, but I wanted to give them more consideration.

First was the water bowl. I already had two water bowls, one in my trailer that was now in Sedona, AZ and the other in my house in Mexico. Being a gypsy, I have homes in two countries, and I need to be able to hold ceremony and have these sacred objects available wherever I am, so I end up needing two sets of everything.

Both of my bowls were purchased, rather than made by me, because I simply don't know enough about working with clay to make my own. They have both been smudged and cleansed and I've used them for my ceremonies. But neither were available to me to bring to the retreat. I decided I would have to go this time without my bowl, knowing that the bowl I had in Sedona had previously been blessed in my first initiation. I decided that the two bowls I have will continue to serve me for my ceremonies until I'm ready to do something different.

I decided I did want a new ceremonial dress. I didn't really like the first one I made and I've always loved sewing. I feel that sewing and crafting is one way that women weave their energy into creation. There's something special in anything we make with love.

I asked myself what a ceremonial dress would look like for me. This ceremony Teri taught us originally comes from a North American tribe, but the tribe is gone. The memory of this ceremony came through for her in meditation and she was bringing it back for women to practice all over the world. So there is no specific clothing or design that goes with the ceremony and we were encouraged to find or make ceremonial regalia that fit for each us, uniquely, as ceremonialists.

So as I contemplated my design I thought of the regalia I've seen worn by North American Indians. While it appealed, I have a much stronger spiritual connection to Mexico than I do the US. And I love the traditional clothing they wear. I wanted something with a Mexican style.

White is commonly worn in ceremony there, with bright red belts and headbands. I like the white, but I've never been one to do the all-white dress. I also love the colorful, embroidered flowers, all handcrafted by Mexican women. But I didn't want to just buy a Mexican dress. So much of the Mexican clothing is gathered and looks very bulky on me. It just doesn't work for my body style. Many of the blouses have puffy sleeves and are too much in the heat.

I live in hot climates most the time. I get uncomfortable in blouses with sleeves, preferring tank tops or sleeveless. I'm also not Mexican and to buy or use their ceremonial dress would have seemed like I was trying to be something I wasn't. I love their culture and I love living there, but I was still not from the country and I didn't want to pretend to be.

So, after a lot of thought and tuning inward, I found a way to blend my tastes with what I love about the Mexican clothes. I made myself a loose-fitting sleeveless blouse using white cotton I had purchased in Mexico. I designed and painted flowers on the top bodice area, similar to the embroidered bodices of the Mexican designs.

I tried it on with a flowered skirt a friend had given me and showed it to Anni. She said the skirt didn't quite work, but she had a straighter cotton knit skirt, if she could find it. So she went digging in her stuff and pulled it out. It was a moss green that matched with the flowers on the bodice and because it was narrow it didn't make me look five sizes bigger than I am. She said I could have it. My outfit was complete.

I also wanted a new talking stick. I loved the talking stick I had in my trailer in Sedona, which I had made for my first initiation. But, I had been renting the trailer out on Airbnb, so it wasn't accessible and Sedona wasn't on my way between California and getting to the ceremony. Plus, I still needed a talking stick for my ceremonies in Mexico, so a new stick would be good to have.

I had a few manzanita sticks in the trunk of my car that I had collected just for this purpose. It was back in winter, when we'd been covering the subject of sacred objects in class while I was hanging out at my friend's house in Nevada City, California. On one of my walks I found a bunch of manzanita had been cut back to clear the brush. I have always loved the smooth red bark of manzanita, so I choose a few sticks to take with me. They'd been in my trunk ever since.

As I was preparing for the retreat I knew I needed to do something to the stick to make it special as my talking stick. I was trying to figure out what that would be.

The weekend before leaving for the retreat I still didn't know what to do. Anni invited me on a camping trip with her family. She brought along some craft projects. While we were hanging out by the fire she pulled out a box of embroidery floss filled with every color imaginable. Anni and the kids started doing macrame. I saw Jordan was using her string to tie around a stick. It sparked an idea. I brought out my stick and began tying it with the colors of the rainbow, fitting for me as the Goddess Ix'Chel is known as Lady of the Rainbow. I tied a few feathers to the end and I had my new stick.

When we returned home I felt prepared and ready for my retreat. I packed my suitcases for Mexico, since I'd be going home after we finished. My daughter, Heidi, and my son-in-law, Dave, said they would store my car for me at their house. A friend was going to give me a ride to the airport the next day so we decided that I'd spend the night at her place. I was ready to go!

CHAPTER 35:

Challenges Getting to Ceremony

EVEN THOUGH I HAD THINGS PLANNED OUT, I was still trying to figure out the logistics. It was complicated. I'd have to drive my car about 20 minutes east, to Heidi's house in Antioch, drop it off and get a ride to BART (the subway system). BART would take me to Walnut Creek, but I'd still need my friend to pick me up, along with all my bags. She lived a couple miles away.

I didn't pack light. I had everything I was taking back to Mexico with me: two suitcases and a duffel to carry on, plus my computer bag. I didn't want to haul all that luggage any more than I had to. And even getting on and off the subway with half as much luggage can be a scramble. To complicate things, I couldn't use Uber, because my Mexican cell phone had almost no memory and I couldn't download the app. And I didn't really want to pay for a cab.

It was around 5:00 pm, almost time to leave if I was going to accomplish all this running around. Even though my flight wasn't until the next day, I needed to coordinate my timing with my friend, Laura, so she could pick me up. But when I called I couldn't get hold of her. I didn't want to get stuck in the evening cold at the Walnut Creek BART Station, just sitting there with all my bags.

Finally, she called. She'd been at the hospital half the night before with her grandson. She was exhausted. He hurt his arm playing football and she had a follow-up appointment with the doctor the next day, right at the time I needed to be at the airport. It was the only time the doctor had available. She couldn't take me. I'd have to figure out other plans.

I was lucky I hadn't yet left the house. I readjusted. One thing gets in the way, it's not a big deal. I can roll with the punches. I'd spend another night at Anni's. I could leave the car where it was and Dave said he'd pick it up later. Anni's son, Jesse, didn't have to work the next day. He had a car. He said could give me a ride all the way to the airport. I wouldn't have to negotiate luggage and BART or any of those other hassles. Everything was perfect!

Until the next day, that is. I wanted to leave around noon. That would give me plenty of time to get to the airport and catch my flight. I was scheduled to arrive in New Mexico a day early. My cousin, Ann, who I had hardly seen in 17 years, was going to pick me up from the airport and spend the day with me. I was really looking forward to seeing her. We'd made the arrangements weeks before, back when I bought the ticket. I'd spend the night at Ann's house and she'd drive me the 30 miles or so to the retreat the following afternoon.

The morning I was to leave, Ann called. It was 11:00 am. I was lucky my computer was still open, because she called on my Skype number. She was suddenly feeling very odd. In fact, she was nauseous and dizzy. She said she'd never felt like this before. She was worried about what could be wrong with her. She had no idea what was going on or what caused it. Perhaps something she ate. She said she might have to go to emergency.

I didn't know what to do. Ann said she couldn't pick me up from the airport. I was arriving at 8:00 pm and all my plans had fallen through. I didn't know anyone else in Albuquerque to call. I asked Ann for her husband's number, thinking that maybe he could help me. I'd never met him, but maybe he could pick me up or figure something out. But Ann was so spaced out that she couldn't even remember her own husband's phone number. I told her I'd figure it out and hung up the phone.

I had to think fast. I was flying Southwest and they are good at transferring tickets, but they charge you the difference if the ticket costs more. I checked their site for prices to change to the following day. They were three or four times what I'd paid. That wasn't going to work.

Next idea. I thought maybe I could just fly in and go directly to the retreat, arriving there a day early. It was being held at Teri's house and I had stayed in her home before, so I that was the next best idea. I tried calling all three of the ladies who were part of helping with the retreat. I knew they were already in town. I couldn't get hold of any of them.

I was running out of time. I needed to leave and get to the airport. I tried calling the retreat leader's husband. He was home. He answered. He said it was fine for me to come early and spend the extra night there, but there wasn't any way they could pick me up from the airport. It was at least a half-hour drive.

He helped me understand the transportation options. Buses were limited, but I found there was a train that ran up that way. It looked like I could barely make the last train, if the timing worked. If I could figure out some way to get to the train from the airport they could pick me up from the station in town. Sounded good. I closed my computer, but left it open to the page with the train schedule.

When I got to the airport I opened it back up to check the train schedule again. I had goofed, been in too much of a hurry. The last train didn't leave Albuquerque at my scheduled arrival time, that was when it arrived in Albuquerque for the night, it was the last stop. No further trains were going anywhere that night.

I had to figure out another plan and do it before I boarded my plane. Otherwise I'd be stuck at the Albuquerque Airport with my four pieces of luggage and nowhere to go. I started looking at Airbnb's. I found some that weren't too expensive. If I could get to them, I'd have a place to sleep and I would have time to catch the train to the retreat in the morning.

Then another miracle came through. There was a lady in our group of ceremonialists, from the prior year of initiates, who was living in Albuquerque and offering to help with rides. I had found her information through a posting on our Facebook group and tried calling her before leaving Anni's, but she hadn't answered her phone so I left a message. As I was waiting for my flight and searching for options, a message popped up from her on Facebook and we connected. She said she'd pick me up and drive all the way there.

As I finally settled into my seat on the plane, I reflected back at all that had transpired to get in my way and yet perfectly align for me to get where I needed to be. Teri had often told us that the bigger your challenges in getting to ceremony, the more powerful the ceremony. I had explained this to people myself when I was booking them on sacred tours and vision quests, but I hadn't experienced anything quite like this. It was my turn. I didn't know what to expect. All I could do was to surrender, turning it over to God/Spirit to guide me and get me where I needed to be. I got the message loud and clear. I was supposed to be at this retreat (a day early even) and it was going to take me deep.

FOREVER 25

CHAPTER 36:

Gabe Shows Up at Ceremony

IT WAS OUR FIRST DAY OF THE RETREAT and by then I'd settled in. The ride went without a hitch and it was great seeing some of my old friends again, as well as meeting new ones.

I got a message late on the night I arrived from my cousin, Ann. When I called her back she gave me the whole story of what happened to her. It wasn't until she was in the hospital emergency that they figured it out. She was hungry and ate some chocolate she found in her fridge. She ate the entire chocolate bar. Her husband must have bought it and left it there. What she didn't know is it had THC in it. He had brought it back from a recent trip to Colorado. This wasn't something they usually did and she's not even a pot smoker, so she didn't pay attention to the label, clearly noting the THC content. When she started feeling the effects she had no idea what was happening. No wonder she was out of it!

Knowing she was better, I was able to leave the world behind and focus on being present and a part of the retreat. I like to tune out from the world and not even check email or phone messages when I'm on retreat. So, now they were all turned off.

Teri opened the ceremony with calling in the feminine spirits and the grandmothers of the ceremony. We would be in ceremony for three days. At the end we would each give away something in our lives and we would make our commitment to this path.

Teri told us how this giveaway would work. She said:

"The giveaway can be anything in your life. I've known people for who their giveaway was very tangible. For one person it was a truck.

"For others it might be a habit or a thought pattern, like an energy they've been holding onto.

"And for some it can be giving away a person, or your attachment to them."

"For example, we had a young woman who was doing her vision quest ceremony. She had invited her mom to be there with her and witness her shift into adulthood. When it was time for the giveaway, her mother gave her away as the daughter she had known. She gave her to herself, to be the adult woman she was now becoming. She let go of her need to take care of her daughter. She let go of needing her daughter to be how she wanted her to be, but to find her way for herself."

These words sunk in. I was in tears as I thought of my son. How could I ever let go of him?

It was time for lunch. We gathered in the kitchen and everyone helped out. Our retreat leader had a southwest style home with the kitchen in the center and the rooms around it, on all sides, almost like a circle.

We moved out to the patio table to eat. My friend, Ariel, who was also the elder for our ceremony, mentioned that her new book would be published and released in September. I was working on her web pages for the book release so I already knew about it. This was her second book and everyone was congratulating her.

I also had my first book almost ready to be published. It was about sacred travel and pilgrimage. I had been a bit more quiet about it. At this point I think I was dallying a bit about getting it published. But I had just gotten it back from my third volunteer editor with all thumbs up. She said she loved the book and had only found a few minor errors. Now fixed, it was as ready as it could get.

I decided to share my news as well. Something about telling about it makes it more real. I had been talking about my pilgrimage book for quite a while. I'd mentioned it to Teri a few years before and she said she was looking forward to reading it, as it might be something she could offer to her people preparing for a vision quest.

But, she also knew I was writing my story about Gabe and she asked how that was coming along. I explained that the book was a bit stuck, but that I hoped to get back to it after publishing the current book. It shifted our conversation to Gabe. My older friends knew about him, but the newer ones did not, so I told them about my son.

Later that day Joy arrived. I hadn't met her before and she hadn't been there for the story about Gabe. She didn't know anything about me. As we were talking she asked me who the spirit was that was hanging out over my left shoulder. This happens a lot in spiritual gatherings with people who are psychic and see things I don't.

I asked Joy to describe the spirit. She said it was a young man and I told her that would have to be my son. Her description matched and when I showed her a picture she said it was definitely him. I wasn't surprised, but it was nice to have someone tell me he was there. I often feel he's close by and like our vision quest, he was here again for our ceremony, even though this one was for women.

We went into back into circle and continued our meditations. Each of us had time with the ceremonial bowl, which represents the womb. I've been in ceremony with this bowl many times throughout the years, but this time was different. It felt like it was pulling me into it. I saw myself standing in the bowl, as water washed over and cleansed me. I touched the bowl and blessed myself with its waters. I could feel Gabe was present with me. When Gabe died, I felt like I'd been torn apart, like it was physically ripping me all the way to my core. Now I felt it was time for healing my womb, where I had held and carried my son. The bowl was representing my womb.

Throughout our meditations I continued to feel this deeper connection to the bowl and the spirits of the ceremony. On our last day we had to do our giveaway. It was time for us to let go of something in our lives. Teri again explained that it could be a material object, perhaps something we may have been too attached to. Or it could even be a person, like letting go of our attachment to our husband or to a child.

I had pondered on what my giveaway would be. It seemed I'd given away so much. What more was there to give? There isn't much that I'm overly attached to any more.

When my turn came, I knew what to do. My giveaway was to give my son back to himself, to let go of my attachment to him and to let go of my need for him to be anything other than who he was. It was so hard to say these words and to let him go. I could barely get out the words.

I stepped into the circle and said: "I give my son, Gabriel Guzman, back to himself, to be his own man, to make his own choices. I release him."

As the ceremony was drawing to a close I saw these pieces of my healing and letting go with Gabe, and I saw them forming a ceremony or ritual that I would do with others. It felt it was part of my calling or purpose. It felt like this was how grieving rituals had been practiced by the native women in their tribe. It was a ceremony for mothers and women, primarily focused on mothers and the healing of their womb. These aspects that I experienced would be a part of it.

And I wanted to bring in the ideas from the movie *Saint Vincent*, simply sharing stories and telling about the loved one(s) we lost. In all the different ways I've talked to people about my son dying, I don't know if anyone asked me what kind of person he was or what he was like. They don't say, "tell me about him." I want to do that, to hold circle, like our talking circles that we do in ceremony, with the focus of simply telling whatever we want to tell about the child we lost.

The beauty of it all is that after searching for a grieving ritual that I felt connected to, now it has simply come to me. Now it is mine to share, from my own experience and what I've endured by losing Gabe.

As the retreat came to an end, after our new initiations, I knew my work was going deeper. I had a new calling, to bring this grieving ritual to the world. There truly had been so much more for me to get and I was so glad I went. These experiences can't happen when you don't show up. It was time for me to find my voice and show up in even bigger ways.

CHAPTER 37:

My Next Chapter of Life

THIS BOOK HAS BEEN AN ONGOING JOURNEY for me. Even though I couldn't do the physical pilgrimage or quest I would have liked, my series of vision quests and ceremonies, combined with my internal exploration, have transformed me inside and out.

I still love walking and do little mini-pilgrimages for a day. I walk in contemplation and with intention. I'm not the same person that I was when Gabe died. His chapter in my life is over while another opens for me.

As I finish this, I'm already moving into new chapters in my life. I just moved from Tlayacapan back to Tepoztlán. When I'd first moved there, almost three years ago, I wanted a new adventure. The small town life in Tepoztlán had gotten to be too gossipy and I thought being away from all the expats would be nice. But, though my Spanish gets me by, I am still not fully conversant and Tlayacapan is a much more traditional town. It doesn't have the hippies and artists and expats and spiritualists that Tepoztlán is filled with. In almost three years living there I never found a connection or friends and I ended up spending most of my time in my concrete box of a house, becoming more isolated than ever.

I still visited Tepoztlán often. It was close, but it took two hours by bus and combis if I was going to the center of town and closer to three hours to go to Amatlán. I had some close friends in both areas and it was my only way to get out with someone for a hike or to simply talk about our lives and socialize. I felt like it was time to be part of the world again and start reaching out to make reconnect and strengthen by friendships and meet new people.

I began to envision the home I wanted for myself. In Tlayacapan I had a very basic house. It was nice inside, but it was a simple concrete box with no yard. It was removed from the jungle and natural world of central Mexico that I'd fallen in love with. My dream home would be surrounded with trees. It would be close to hiking trails or places to walk and explore. I wanted it close to town, but not in the noisy areas where fiestas and loud music were a regular thing.

I'd seen a house for rent on Tepoztlán's Facebook page and when I came back from summer in California I went to see it. I fell in love! It felt as if it had been made just for me. It's an adobe and stone house, surrounded by garden and trees. And easy to get to the combi and into town. Yet it's quiet and away from the busyness of town. It's a place I can hold ceremony again.

Life in the US is ready for a change as well. I'm hoping to move my RV back to either the mountains or somewhere closer to my kids. I'm ready for an easier life. I've simplified enough, now I'm ready to expand and feel spacious.

A few months ago, before I left California to come back to Mexico, I got invited by Loretta Masnada, one of the Blue Star moms that had Gabe's plaque made, to join her at an Eagle Scout Awards Ceremony for Ryan Darner, a young man that had made it his Eagle Scout project to beautify the area around Gabe's plaque. I saw a bit of my son in this handsome young man, this boy who never met Gabe or Mick or Scott, but decided our sons' lives were worth remembering. Thanks to Loretta and Carol, our sons are being remembered.

And in this new chapter of my life, I finally got to meet some of Gabe's comrades, in November 2019. That spring, as I was writing this book, I was thinking about how much I'd like to know the people he served with, especially those he considered friends. Then, out of the blue, I got an email from Charlie Company that they were having a Warrior Reunion in Texas in November and were inviting all the Gold Star Families. They offered to fly us in and take care of everything. As I finished this book, I was looking forward to getting to know these men and hear their stories.

If I ever write another book, it will probably be a bunch of individual pieces of conversations I've had with soldiers who have come home. Their story is an important one as well.

Gabe's death shattered my illusions of life. It has taken me to places I wouldn't have chosen to go, but it has shown me so much through my challenges and sorrow. In facing the truth of who I am, at the depths of my shadows and fears, I have found my inner strength and beauty.

Now I search out friends who will join me in going deep and facing life as it is. I'm no longer interested in superficial encounters. I want connection, but not the shallow interchange where most people dwell. I like to talk about real stuff. I tell my friends that Gabe's death is still hard on me and hurts. I don't agree with ideas like *"Heaven needed another angel,"* certainly not more than we needed him here. I won't settle for platitudes.

I have less patience for people who spew out complaints of someone sitting too close on the bus or getting in their way in line. It's hard for me to be around people with judgments and assumptions. One day I overheard a friend making fun of someone with one arm. I wish my son were here with only an arm blown off. And living in near-third-world environments I have very little patience for the "first-world complaints."

Yet, I do have more compassion for people than ever before, especially those who have been through challenges and found their way by discovering an inner strength. I have compassion for people at any place along their path. If I can help them find their own strength by letting them know they aren't alone and that someone else cares, I have made the world a better place. But even if we just hang out and mutually enjoy each other, that is enough.

I realize that we can only be there for others at the level we've learned for ourselves and we're all just doing the best we can to get through this mess we call life. I try to see what others are going through, even the parts they aren't showing the world.

So much of our upbringing and conditioning taught us to push away the bad things and especially topics such as death. My mother, who didn't hear the words I tried to say, grew up without her own mother. My real grandma died when my mom was young. I can't imagine how difficult that would be for her. She had to get on with life and was raised by a very loving step-mother. But I think if anything comes close or matches the pain of losing a child, it would be losing a parent at a young age. I know that my mom loves me and I love her. And I still try to work past my own conditioning and use this lesson to listen better when others are in pain.

I'm ready to take what I've learned further out in the world. I'd love to see a world where we can honor and celebrate a person's life with ceremony and ritual. We need to accept grief and the emotions that go with it and talk about it instead of shutting it away. I'm getting ready to start offering grieving circles and healing rituals for others, as places we can support each other and simply tell our stories and listen.

I think back on my journey. I needed to find my way, in my own way. By the time I moved away from Tlayacapan, I had started feeling my home there was like a jail cell, and I was so ready to get away from there and move to somewhere new. But the time of being alone and isolated was good for me as well, like being in the womb. I needed to go inward. Now it's my time to go outward and share my love, my heart and my gifts with others who need a bit of what I needed, someone else to listen and care.

Acknowledgements

I would like to thank those who helped me in getting this book published.

First, my Patreon supporters made all the difference. They not only supported the process, but they stuck with me and encouraged me for the three years it took me to write it, some all the way from start to finish.

My Patreaon supporters are: Melissa Brown Blaeuer, Lark Tucker, Colette Cunningham, Victoria Markham, Kim Snowden, Paul Sowell, Sean Kelly, Chaya Bush, and Lorna McCarthy.

Their contributions, whether for a month or the full three years helped me see that this story was important, not just for me but for all those who would read and share it. Our stories need to be told.

These words from Melissa Brown Blaeuer were the kind of support that kept me going when I was often ready to quit:

"You are on a wonderful and healing journey toward feeling complete about what your family has been through. I think what you're writing about is really important, and will touch many, many people personally, for the better. Let the healing begin."

My Patrons contributions also helped me be a better writer and turn memories in memoir. Because of them, I was able pay for courses on writing story and memoir. One was an online writing course by Joyce Maynard on Writing Memoir. After listening, re-watching the videos and studying all that she taught, she is now one of the voices in my head, prompting me along. I got so much help from this course. Thank you, Joyce.

I've also been encouraged by the feedback of my Facebook friends and family. Knowing that my writing is touching others helps me see our connectedness and how my joy and pain can also bring understanding to others.

I thank all the characters in the story for all they've brought to my life.

I'd like to thank all those who helped in the editing process, especially my friend Edward Mason. Edward brought the needed perspective and corrections to see what I missed and polish the story for completion. As a friend, he's also been there to listen to my story in shared hours of conversation including our thoughts of death, war, and how the loss of a child has affected our lives. Thank you, Edward for your help, your friendship and your professional eye.

Finally, I have to thank my son, Gabe, for choosing me to be his mother. For all the time we did have together and all that we've shared. Gabe brought so much to my life that has enriched me forever.

About the Author

Ixchel Tucker (born and known by her family as Shelley Tucker*) is a spiritual guide, mentor, teacher, ceremonialist and writer and author of the new book: *"Forever 25: A Mother's Journey through Grief."*

As a freelance website and graphic designer, Ixchel has written numerous blog and magazine articles in the area of travel, sacred sites, sacred feminine practices, spiritual awakening, and personal transformation.

Her son, Gabriel Guzman, was killed by a roadside bomb while on patrol in Afghanistan in 2008. Her book, *"Forever 25"*, is the story of her journey, to transform her grief, while still carrying all the love of her son, Gabe, into all areas of her life.

Ixchel *(or Shelley)* has traveled around parts of Europe, the US, and Mexico. Her search for her true self has led her to explore her inner world through Vision Quests and indigenous ceremonies. At the same time she developed a passion for sacred sites around the world, where she found an awakening between her outer world and inner knowing.

Her life is one of continual learning and evolving. She completed a year-long apprenticeship in leading Ceremonial Leadership and the Sacred Feminine and a deeper course in Spiritual Ministry. Additionally, she has worked for spiritual leaders including Neale Donald Walsch, James Twyman, Misa Hopkins, Finbarr Ross and others.

Ixchel has a gyspy-spirit that keeps her moving and exploring. Following an inner guidance she moved to Mexico in 2006 where she now lives part of the year, with the balance of her time in the California Bay Area with her family. She has a love the outdoors, traveling, hiking, and dancing, connecting with people and meeting new friends.

She choose to write this book under her birth name, Shelley Tucker, simply because her son never would have acknowledged her by any other name.

Also by Ixchel Tucker

Ixchel is also author of two other books:

The Pilgrim's Way - Become the Master of Your Spiritual Adventure

Magic Comes Alive in Mexico - An Adventure of Self Discovery.

Ixchel is also author of numerous blog articles about Sacred Travel, Self Discovery, and Traveling in Mexico.

Her websites are:
adventurequestsintl.com
mexicosmagicdestinations.com
forever25.us

Ixchel (*aka: Shelley*) likes photos and to see the people in memoirs, to put a face to a name and images of the places where a story took place.

For photos and images, you can visit
Forever25.us/gallery

or the Facebook page:
facebook.com/Ixchel.Tucker25